DIFFICULT

decisions

ERIC PLINER

CEO of YSC Consulting

DIFFICULT
decisions

How Leaders
Make the Right Call
with Insight, Integrity,
and Empathy

WILEY

Published by John Wiley & Sons, Inc., Hoboken, New Jersey.
Published simultaneously in Canada.

For general information on our other products and services or for technical support, please contact our Customer Care Department within the United States at (800) 762-2974, outside the United States at (317) 572-3993 or fax (317) 572-4002.

Wiley publishes in a variety of print and electronic formats and by print-on-demand. Some material included with standard print versions of this book may not be included in e-books or in print-on-demand. If this book refers to media such as a CD or DVD that is not included in the version you purchased, you may download this material at http://booksupport.wiley.com. For more information about Wiley products, visit www.wiley.com.

Library of Congress Cataloging-in-Publication Data:

Names: Pliner, Eric, author.
Title: Difficult decisions : how leaders make the right call with insight, integrity, and empathy / Eric Pliner.
Description: Hoboken, New Jersey : Wiley, [2022] | Includes index.
Identifiers: LCCN 2021062105 (print) | LCCN 2021062106 (ebook) | ISBN 9781119817048 (cloth) | ISBN 9781119817086 (adobe pdf) | ISBN 9781119817062 (epub)
Subjects: LCSH: Decision making. | Leadership.
Classification: LCC HD30.23 .P554 2022 (print) | LCC HD30.23 (ebook) | DDC 658.4/03—dc23/eng/20220118
LC record available at https://lccn.loc.gov/2021062105
LC ebook record available at https://lccn.loc.gov/2021062106

Cover image: © Getty Images | Miragec
Cover design: Paul McCarthy
SKY10032492_020422

For Jonathan

Contents

Preface: Writing Wrong   xi

Chapter 1 Difficult Decisions   1

    Making Difficult Decisions   8

    How We Make Decisions Now   11

    Key Points   22

Chapter 2 The Moral–Ethical–Role Responsibility
Triangle   23

    Morals versus Ethics: *Election*   27

    Jean and Paula   29

    Win as Much as You Can   32

    Do the Right Thing   41

    Key Points   42

Chapter 3 Morals   43

    Communicating Your Morality and
      Asking about Morality   47

    Knowing the Sources of Your Morality 54

      Reflecting on the Sources of Your
      Morality   55

      Understanding the Parameters and
      Boundaries of Your Morality 56

A Moral Exercise   67

Exercise: Morality and Your Leadership
    Narrative   70

Key Points   73

Chapter 4 Ethics   75

Characteristics of Ethics   77
    Ethics Are Contextually Dependent and
        Are, Therefore, Not Uniform   77
    Ethics Can Change over Time   81
    Ethics Are about Shared Social
        Acceptability, but They Are Not
        about Popularity   83

The Ethics of Leading Politically   92

Waiving Ethics   95
    An Exercise in Exceptions   98

Ethics and Judgment   100

An Ethics Exercise   102

Key Points   111

Chapter 5 Role Responsibilities   113

Who You Are Charged to Serve   117
    Stakeholder Mapping   118
    Socioemotional Role   121
    Understanding Dynamic Roles   128

A Role Exercise   137

Key Points   145

Chapter 6 Using the Triangle to Make Difficult
            Decisions   147

Decision-Making Ecosystem and Its
    Associated Expectations   148

Thoughtful Learning and Development
    for the Leader   149
The Importance of Deep Consideration
    of What Truly Matters to Us   149
What and How to Communicate to
    Audiences with Varied Needs and
    Perspectives   150

The Tissue Test   153

Key Points   161

Chapter 7 I Think I Know What I Think;
                     Now What?   163

A Decision-Making Process   164

A View, a Voice, a Vote, or a Veto   180
    A View   181
    A Voice   182
    A Vote   182
    A Veto   183

Delegating   184

Facts versus Feelings   186

Tools and Muscles   187

Key Points   190

Afterword   191

Acknowledgments   193

About the Author   197

Index   199

Preface

Writing Wrong

This book is wrong.

I don't mean that it's bad or evil. I mean that it's inevitably incorrect.

There is content within these pages with which you are bound to disagree. Your view isn't necessarily right; but then, neither is mine. Nevertheless, some of what I have to say is undoubtedly just plain wrong.

Much of what is contained herein has been examined in various settings for literal millennia. And still—or perhaps inevitably—not everyone sees it the same way. For instance, one fundamental tenet of this book's core framework—that morals are internally referenced and externally influenced, while ethics are externally referenced and distilled internally—runs in direct contradiction to the starting point of plenty of brilliant thinkers in the field. (A pair of ethicists, one in the UK and one in Australia, use definitions in their shared writing that are almost exactly opposite to mine.)[1]

[1] Paul Walker and Terry Lovat, "You Say Morals, I Say Ethics—What's the Difference?" *The Conversation*, September 18, 2014. https://theconversation.com/you-say-morals-i-say-ethics-whats-the-difference-30913.

Discussions of right and wrong, of good and evil, of fairness and injustice are all deeply personal; they are also contextual and time bound. As a result, some of what I write with certainty today (and much of what I write with uncertainty) is bound to be easily discarded, depending on things like where and when you live, how you are encountering this text, and your reasons for reading it. That is the paradox of insisting that how we make the most difficult decisions must always be contextual.

Add to this the complication of your specific, current leadership context, with responsibility for the well-being, satisfaction, engagement, productivity, happiness, or work/life conditions of an increasingly crowded array of stakeholders, plus the fact that morality and ethics are inherently subjective and ever-evolving, as is our understanding of what it means to lead. All that complexity equals a high degree of likelihood that this book doesn't have clear answers, that it's wrong, or that the apparent answers that seem clear and right today will seem muddy and incorrect far sooner than I or my publisher would like.

I still think it's worth writing, and hopefully you still think it's worth reading. Here's why.

We define *leadership strategy* as the intentional design of the individual styles, the dynamics and interactions, and the collective cultures that create the conditions for others to deliver desired change. Whether that desired change is increased profit or market share, entry into a new geography, election of a new office holder to state or federal government, development of a new and evocative artistic experience, corralling community resources for greater equity in their distribution, or something else entirely, leaders make it possible ("create the conditions") for people working together ("others") to drive results, outcomes, or impact ("deliver desired change"). That's a tall task, and it's one that's best not left to chance ("intentional design"). After all, we have organizational strategies and financial strategies— why wouldn't we have leadership strategies, too?

Intentional design of those leadership strategies requires understanding where we've come from, who and where we are today, how we got here, where we want to go, and how we'd like to get there. That's the part where thinking about how to make the most difficult decisions before we're actually faced with them has the most potential to be useful. Given the sheer number of difficult decisions that leaders have to make every day, the pace required of that decision-making, and the seemingly higher and higher stakes of those decisions, clarifying an approach by design rather than by default leaves us more ready to deal with challenges we've never encountered previously—like a global pandemic or unprecedented economic disruption or irreversible changes to our physical climate or a woefully unreliable supply chain or bans on international travel or the *en masse* theft of customer data or the disruption of democracy or whatever the next year brings, or the one after that.

Doing so also helps to prepare us to tackle difficult decisions that we haven't considered because we don't know anything about them just yet, which means that we also don't know anything about their answers, which is why the approach in this book is probably wrong or at least ill-suited to some of the tough questions that we're bound to face.

One thing is for sure: I'm not going to tell you what's moral, what's ethical, or what your role is as a leader. I'm not going to tell you what's right or wrong, helpful or harmful, or who your stakeholders are. These are highly subjective questions with context-specific answers. Our aspirations to objectivity in any of these matters are merely pretensions, likely imbued with personal experiences and ways of living in the world that are so core to who we are that we hardly notice them anymore.

With that in mind, I'm not going to try to persuade you about my particular views, nor am I going to go overboard in sharing my expertise. Hopefully, this book will help you to unpack your own expertise and to understand your own views with greater skill and sophistication. Hopefully, you will find a path to more intentional application of what matters to you by figuring out with greater clarity exactly what matters to you. Hopefully, the exercises here will help you to understand the realities that become manifest through your opinions and perspectives and the identities and experiences that inform them.

My desire to focus on understanding your opinions and perspective is in no way intended to suggest that I don't believe in facts—or their importance. After years of working in the behavioral sciences, I suspect that not everything that we classify as science constitutes permanently resolved fact. It only takes a cursory review of the lack of replicability of many classic experiments in psychology with well-accepted findings to illuminate that point. By contrast, faults in our earlier understanding and the healthy evolution of our thinking do not negate the existence of facts. Instead, they reflect the importance of lifelong learning and openness to new information. Our prior collective certainty that the Earth was flat does not make it any less round.

What I am concerned with is how, as leaders, we interpret the world around us based on our current knowledge and what we do with that interpretation. How do we use our understanding of good and bad to enrich the quality of our lives and of life on Earth more generally and to leave the world better than we found it? Several of these words—*good*, *bad*, *enrich*, *quality*, *better*—are far from value-agnostic in their definitions. As leaders, we make choices many times each day that impose our interpretation of these words on others. Responsible leadership, therefore, begs our thoughtful consideration of these words and their related concepts, of the sources of our interpretations, and of the impact of our interpretations on others who may or may not share them.

Right or wrong, whatever this approach represents, at least it's by design and not by accident.

Hopefully, you will leave this reading having reflected on where you've come from, who and where you are today, and how you got here. Hopefully, you will have considered where you want to go next, both as an individual and as a leader, and how you'd like to get there. Hopefully, you will design a plan and approach to complex personal and professional challenges with intent, enabling you to make tough choices with insight, integrity, and empathy. And hopefully, you will get to do so well ahead of the next round of pain inherent in making the most difficult leadership decisions: the ones that highlight our conflicts, our contradictions, and our hypocrisies, yes—but also our humanity and our ability to shape the future.

You're going to want to grab a pen and some paper. Some of this might hurt a little bit. At the very least, maybe you'll be more ready for whatever is waiting for you tomorrow. If not, well, don't worry. This book is probably wrong anyway.

Eric Pliner
September 2021

Epigraph

Life is pain, Highness. Anyone who says differently is selling something.
>   —The Man in Black in *The Princess Bride*
>   by William Goldman

1

Difficult Decisions

I had been in the role of chief executive officer of YSC Consulting, a 30-year-old, global leadership strategy firm, for about two years when one of our client teams approached me with a dilemma.

Sixteen months after we felt the first economic effects of COVID-19, our financial performance had returned successfully to its pre-pandemic levels. Still, like many businesses around the world, we remained only a few months removed from worrying whether our boutique consultancy would survive the economic and health crises imposed by the pandemic. The climb back to strong earnings had been arduous and exhausting, and our attention was heightened to every possible opportunity to maintain our recovery and growth.

Everyone was pleased, then, when one of our longstanding partners moved to a new company – this time, a defense contractor and manufacturer – and called on our client team for support. Our contact's new organization needed help shaping their approaches to leadership succession and to diversity, equity, and inclusion, the confluence of which represented one of our firm's sweet spots. The client anticipated a sizable contract, enough to close a gap in forecast performance for the region, and knew that our capabilities were a strong match for the organization's need. Our team went to work immediately, using their knowledge of the client, the industry, and the current moment to craft a custom solution that matched the caller's circumstances precisely – exactly what any great consulting firm would do.

But when Cara, a member of our administrative team, proofread the proposal, she was uneasy. She'd used a superior set of research skills to dig into the gap between the company's carefully curated public image and less savory activities that independent media outlets had reported more recently. Cara was concerned that we were compromising our values in service of the potential opportunity.

We were no strangers to working with complex or controversial industries; our client portfolio included tobacco companies, oil and gas companies with known histories of environmental damage, pharmaceutical manufacturers sued for artificially raising prices of drugs to treat rare disease, low-end retailers accused of exploiting rural communities, financial services organizations that had settled extensive claims resulting from the sale of mortgage-backed securities, and plenty of others. As leadership strategists, our work helps organizations to design their desired leadership styles, interactions and dynamics, and organizational cultures with intent, rather than leaving those critical human elements to default. Incorporating thoughtfully designed values, expectations of sustainability, awareness of community and environmental impact, and deep understanding of the constellation of organizational stakeholders is at the heart of what we do, and so we embrace opportunities to help leaders, teams, and organizations to make changes to their strategies or operations to lead with integrity, pride, and resolve. These particularly challenging scenarios were among those where our work was most impactful and most rewarding. But this one felt different.

Cara's discomfort was on my mind, but I'd heard plenty of discomfort before. We'd made the collective decision to encourage our colleagues to opt out of participating in any project or account with which they felt personally misaligned, and that practice had worked successfully to date, without compromise to the business. She wasn't asking to step away from the project, though; she was asking that the firm make a choice to turn down the opportunity and the partnership entirely.

We had to weigh another element, one that reflected our ethical context. Without a doubt, Cara's thinking was informed by an experience in our professional community that had brought us closer together. In the fall of 2019, we'd licensed the TED platform for use at an internal, all-company meeting. Speaker after speaker blended original research, cutting-edge ideas, and personal experiences to spread ideas about leadership, business, and our firm with passion and power. As one well-loved colleague – a particularly powerful speaker – shared her childhood experience as a refugee from civil war in vivid detail, the room hardly moved. Over the subsequent days, the business worked together to turn our co-workers' rich ideas and personal narratives into decisions about organizational practices and our desired future. Deciding that we wouldn't work with organizations that manufactured and/or sold weapons of war was relatively straightforward; we had few if any clients that met those criteria anyway, and our colleague's message was undeniable.

On a personal level, I didn't take that stance lightly. While I hold a degree in peace and justice studies, my father was a career civil servant for branches of the US military prior to joining a private-sector firm that contracted with those same agencies. We'd had a version of these discussions and debates around our family dinner table for decades, often agreeing to accept that our conversations were unlikely to be closed or resolved in any meaningful way.

Nevertheless, the firm had held this decision with real pride and shared it publicly, fully considering the possibility that we might countenance a version of this exact dilemma in the future: the opportunity to deliver meaningful work to people who wanted it, needed it, asked for it, and were prepared to pay for it, but with whom we could not align our values. We'd opted to employ what some call an "abundance mindset,"[1] the belief that ample opportunity in the marketplace would allow us to readily find work that we wanted to deliver, in line with our values and cultural priorities. Essentially, we were confident that we'd never need to take on work that hurt in the ways that we'd identified.

What we hadn't accounted for, though, was an unanticipated and drastic shift in context that created a conflict between our morality and our role responsibilities as leaders and service providers. The world had changed since we'd determined that we could turn away prospective

---

[1] Caroline Castrillon, "5 Ways to Go from a Scarcity to Abundance Mindset," *Forbes*. July 12, 2020. https://www.forbes.com/sites/carolinecastrillon/2020/07/12/5-ways-to-go-from-a-scarcity-to-abundance-mindset/?sh=2e6366ce1197.

revenue. Neither our survival as a firm nor our ability to fully employ our people – many of whom relied on us for health care for themselves and their families – were guaranteed. Perhaps they never had been, but years of strong performance had left these existential questions well out of sight. But after a year where nearly every organization in our industry had laid off employees, reduced compensation, restricted hiring, closed offices, defaulted on financial obligations, or taken other measures to save cost in exchange for protecting their organizations and the majority of their people, turning down a large contract with guaranteed revenue – thereby potentially putting some of our people, their livelihood, and their families at risk – seemed irresponsible, if not downright unethical.

Simultaneously, the client organizations and their leaders who sought support from us, some of whom we were meeting for the first time, were also in new waters. Every organization we encountered was grappling with often unprecedented leadership dilemmas about right and wrong, good and bad, survival and destruction, wellness and illness, diversity and similarity, speed and deliberateness, short-term and long-term needs, even life and death. And few of them had the luxury of time to seek a wide range of perspectives; they wanted perspective, support, coaching, and thought partnership from trusted advisors, which we are, and they needed these supports urgently.

We were clear about the belief that our work delivers meaningful impact and helps leaders and organizations to shape a desirable future; we'd found a way to balance it with the belief that we did not want to cause further harm to our community members or to the world, and we backed that up by not supporting the manufacture and sale of weapons of war. We held the unshakable belief that accepting an organization as our client makes us responsible to be of service to them; our role is to provide them with experiences and support to ensure intentional design of the leadership styles, interpersonal dynamics, and cultures that enable successful achievement of strategy. Although we hadn't thought of it quite so dramatically in the hardy years prior to COVID, we also held the fervent belief that our ability to sustain our firm, to meet our financial obligations, and to employ our people without compromise to their livelihood, their families, and their health care, was good for them, good for the world, and good for business. Now that these criticalities were no longer guaranteed in the ways that we had naively assumed, it was incumbent upon us as leaders to consider the conflict anew.

At first glance, this apparent dilemma sounds like a textbook display of an oft-levied accusation against private-sector organizations and leaders: The moment that financial performance is challenged, values go out the window. But scratching the surface only slightly reveals that this paradigm is not, in fact, present in the most stereotypical way – and almost never is.

The real conflict is between competing dimensions of personal morality, ethical context, and the role responsibilities of the leader – all of which exist in service of good.

So, is it right to turn away revenue that might protect employment, compensation, and benefits during a period of macroeconomic uncertainty and high unemployment? What if completing activities to earn that revenue runs counter to the psychological contract explicitly agreed with the moral view of the organization's employees? On the other hand, what if engaging in these activities furthers the organization's ethical position – about helping leaders of all kinds to make good judgments and to use their drive and influencing skill to shape the future?

In her book *How to Wow: Proven Strategies for Selling Your [Brilliant] Self in Any Situation*, author Frances Cole Jones asks herself and her readers, "Do you want to be right, or do you want to be friends?"[2] It's a straightforward question that begs deeper exploration: What matters most? Intellectual integrity or real relationships? Holding on to our ideas or holding on to other people?

The answer, of course, is both. People and principles are inextricably linked, and it is nonetheless often impossible to make everyday decisions that attend to both with equal passion.

Over and again, leaders are called upon to make complex decisions quickly in ways that fulfill the responsibilities of our roles, that are in line with the ethical expectations of our sociocultural context, and that match our personal morality. The most difficult decisions cannot be made objectively, no matter how many analytics we complete. But understanding the sources of our views, examining rather than blindly accepting our feelings and obligations across stakeholder audiences, and knowing the pressures and incentives of the contexts in which we operate can enable us to make tough calls successfully.

That doesn't mean that there won't be trade-offs and that everyone will be happy with our choices.

Ultimately, I signed the contract, and we took the organization in question into our portfolio as a client. You might stop reading now, convinced that my team and I sold out, that we made an immoral choice to prioritize profit over people, to place our shareholders' interests above our ostensible values. I've considered that possibility plenty of times – both before making the call and since. But the simple

---

[2] Frances Cole Jones, *How to Wow: Proven Strategies for Selling Your [Brilliant] Self in Any Situation* (New York: Ballantine Books, 2008).

action of scribbling my name on a tablet screen belied the hours of self-reflection, team discussion, open debate, process consideration, research, and values clarification that went into making this difficult decision. Confronted with an array of options and a seemingly endless mix of opinions, I am confident that we made the right choice for our firm and our people. We didn't avoid the apparent conflict between our roles as leaders, our personal codes of morality, and the ethical context in which we operate, even (especially) where those dimensions were misaligned. We indulged the challenge, clarified how we would choose, explored the factors driving us toward and away from each potential outcome, and made a difficult decision with insight, empathy, and integrity.

Making Difficult Decisions

How many decisions do you make each day?
What's the toughest decision you've had to make?
Why was it so hard?
How did you ultimately make the call?
Did you get it right?
How do you know?

Our most difficult choices rarely challenge us because we lack information. They're not solved by aggregating data or reviewing spreadsheets or even by using artificial intelligence.

Our most difficult decisions challenge us because they dig at some raw aspect of our humanity: what we believe in our hearts about right and wrong; our hopes and fears about how others will respond to us; and our desire to be good people and to leave legacies that reflect who we believe ourselves to be. They challenge us because they require us to confront conflicts between what we think and what we do, between our view of ourselves as inherently good and choices that mean that not everyone will experience us as good. They require us to recognize that there are few absolutes and lots of nuances. And they require us to recognize that, as the heroes of our own life narratives, we are sometimes the villains in others' life narratives.

By its very nature, leadership – that is, creating the conditions for change in service of generating shared value and meaning – is inherently interpersonal. It requires bringing people together to envision and enable a future that is somehow different from today. Leaders prompt personal and communal growth and development; generate emotional soothing and comfort; inspire new perspectives and ways of being; engender individual, collective, and community wellness, health, and wealth; and help us to know and understand who we are and why we are here.

And because leadership is interpersonal, how we lead today affects real people's real lives right now – and may have consequences for years and even generations to come.

There is a lot for leaders to learn about the sources of and context for our choices, and there is a lot that all of us can learn from other leaders to inform how we make the most difficult decisions of our lives.

Leadership is about tough choices, and making tough choices shows leadership.

We must ask ourselves, then, what kind of leadership we want to show. What kind of leaders – and people – do we want to be? And how does thoughtful, considered conscientiousness and communication about these choices make us better at what we do – and who we are?

It doesn't matter if you think these decisions are right or if anyone agrees – the whole point is that lots of people don't and won't agree. That's what makes these decisions difficult. They are subjective, and subjective decision-making is not helped by pretending to objectivity. We can't do it. We're human, we're fallible. Our lives, identities, and experiences shape the way we see the world. There's no such thing as human objectivity. So then, we want to look to science. Science, after all, can be objective. There are hard facts in the world of science. We follow the impulse to want to rely on something seemingly scientific, seemingly objective. And so we look to things like machine learning and artificial intelligence, hoping that they can somehow tell us what to do about the hard stuff, either forgetting that these technologies are themselves still created and programmed by humans (with all of our biases and fallibilities) and ignoring the fact that they still can't tell us what to do about the really hard stuff – the subjective stuff. An algorithm can give us answers – perhaps even the best answers that do the least harm – but it cannot tell us how a group of humans, each with different backgrounds and identities and experiences, will feel about those answers. And that means that perhaps it hasn't given us answers at all.

There is ample and increasing evidence that the best decisions are made by so-called centaurs[3] – part human, part machine – building on the superior analytical capability (and, perhaps more importantly, speed) of technologies and the essential empathy and experience-based intuition of humans.

But they still can't tell us how to feel or what to do when we think something is just plain wrong. That requires us to rely on our judgment – the blend of spotting and recognizing issues (anticipating and responding to the practical environment decisively and realistically); the rigor of our

---

[3] Kevin Yamazaki, "Reconciling the AI-human conflict with the centaur model," *CIO Review* (n.d.), https://artificial-intelligence.cioreview.com/cxoinsight/reconciling-the-aihuman-conflict-with-the-centaur-model-nid-24514-cid-175.html.

cognition (processing and making sense of complexity, insight, and nuance in a balanced way); and framing (seeing broader themes and perspectives, distilling clarity from ambiguity). Our ability to make those judgments skillfully is informed by what's going on inside of us, what's going on around us, and what we understand is expected of us.

So rather than looking for ways to make decisions more objectively, every one of us who has a difficult choice to make should instead focus on how to build and sharpen the ability to make subjective decisions with greater skill.

How We Make Decisions Now

Plenty of decision-making frameworks implore leaders to use seemingly objective information more thoughtfully, and seek to help individuals to mitigate bias,[4] decide differently in the moment versus over time,[5] or make rigorous use of data.[6] We've established that these models are less direct in addressing the equal complexity and tremendous importance of the intentionally subjective aspects of leadership decision-making. The notion of making "good" decisions – a demand of every leadership role – is addressed in part by understanding our sources for making subjective decisions and by finding ways to ensure integrity among them – especially when these sources are in apparent conflict.

---

[4] Yunfeng Zhang, Rachel K.E. Bellamy, and Wendy A. Kellogg, "Designing Information for Remediating Cognitive Biases in Decision-Making," Proceedings of the 33rd Annual ACM Conference on Human Factors in Computing Systems, April 2015, 2211–2220, https://dl.acm.org/doi/abs/10.1145/2702123.2702239.

[5] Michael Kirchler et al., "The effect of fast and slow decisions on risk taking," *Journal of Risk and Uncertainty*, June 7, 2017, 37–59. https://link.springer.com/article/10.1007/s11166-017-9252-4.

[6] Erik Brynjolfsson, Lorin M. Hitt, and Heekyung Hellen Kim, "Strength in Numbers: How Does Data-Driven Decisionmaking Affect Firm Performance?" *SSRN*, December 12, 2011, DOI: 10.2139/ssrn.1819486.

For starters, every leadership decision is imbued with both ethics (contextual principles about what is acceptable in our organizations and our societies) and morals (our own internal sense of what is right and what is wrong, shaped by upbringing, family, community, identity, faith, and more).

"But wait," you say, "aren't ethics and morals synonymous and, you know, interchangeable?" Plenty of thinkers, writers, and philosophers will tell us why one can be substituted for the other, or at least how closely they are related. For all of their overlap, though, differentiating between morals and ethics gives us important data about how we personally understand what is right and what is wrong, and how our context evaluates the relative helpfulness or harmfulness of specific actions.

There's a Whitney Houston song whose title puts it even more simply: "It's Not Right, But It's Okay." The action is morally wrong, yes, but limited in harm and therefore generally acceptable (or at least not unacceptable).

All of this is complicated by the leader's understanding of the responsibilities of their role in a complex operating context: for and on behalf of whom am I working? Carefully interrogating these three dimensions enables the leader to make the best possible decisions in service of addressing the many, varied needs of a constellation of stakeholders.

As our operating context changes – and it is changing faster than ever before – it is incumbent upon every leader to clarify their understanding of the evolving ethical framework that said context demands. For instance, as recently as a few years ago, an apolitical approach to social controversy was broadly perceived as the right ethical framework for leaders; today, many employees and consumers demand that their leaders take a strong stance on complex issues that are of importance to them. And since those employees and consumers don't generally hold identical views themselves, a leader who appears to be political inevitably satisfies some stakeholders and alienates others.

The leader's impulse, then, might be to shy away from taking any potentially controversial stances, but that doesn't work either; fairly or not, our current ethical context interprets silence or inaction as an opinion in and of itself.

As a personal sense of right and wrong is also a driver of decision-making, considering the development of one's own morality and the source of its influences is essential. How might someone with a different upbringing, set of life experiences, personal or family values, or educational influences perceive the same question differently? Not incidentally, this is among the strong arguments for surrounding oneself with a diverse team and cultivating an inclusive and psychologically safe culture that elicits these perspectives as a matter of course.

Perhaps most obviously, clarifying the requirements and expectations of one's role is essential. Is the leader obligated to all stakeholders equally? What results do shareholders expect, and do their expectations outweigh those of others in the stakeholder constellation? Should employees, customers, and communities be treated with the same regard as owners and investors? And what happens when these needs are in conflict?

For instance, consider a CEO facing the decision of whether to lay off employees in a recession. Filtered through the lens of morality, she might feel that taking away an individual's livelihood at such a time would be immoral. Ethics, however, demand that leaders sacrifice the well-being of a few individuals to protect the rest of the organization. If she believes her role requires her to protect the interests of as many of the organization's key stakeholders as possible – including shareholders, employees, customers, and community members – then her determination about whether her job demands laying off employees might seem inherently conflicted. Accordingly, her role requirements align with ethics, even where her personal morality diverges. This apparent congruence of only two dimensions leaves the CEO with two acceptable options:

1. Explicitly leverage the influence that accompanies her role to transparently attempt to persuade key stakeholders to align expectations of her role with her personal morality.
2. Sacrifice her individual views for the greater good implied at the intersection of collective ethics and her role responsibilities.

Following her morals despite a conflict with her role will get her fired, so that's not in the option set here. The available choices are to use her morality to influence the expectations of her role or to decide to sacrifice her morality; either option requires reconciliation or acceptance of divergent views.

A hiring manager may know that his role demands protecting the financial, social, and structural interests of his institution by ensuring the placement of the best possible candidate in each position in his part of the organization. His personal morals might suggest that all individuals in a work setting should be judged based solely on the quality of their work, and not on their social identities – ability status, country of origin, gender identity, race, religion, sex, or sexual orientation, among others. And his ethical context might suggest that a meritocratic system is the fairest, aligning his morals and ethics in service of his role. However, as collective ethics shift to embrace a broader understanding that ostensibly meritocratic employment systems do not account for educational or structural disparities or the intangible value of lived experience among those holding marginalized identities, he might find that his role and ethical context align to supersede his personal morals. Such alignment enables clarity of decision-making, and may also, in some cases, lead to a reevaluation of said morality.

Board chairs know that they are responsible for representing the interests of shareholders, bar none. Although these interests are not exclusively financial, the board's role in governance is generally clear. In the case of a CEO accused of one or more extramarital relationships, the board chair's personal morality may identify adultery as wrong; conversely, it may indicate that extramarital relationships are private matters only. Neither of these views is relevant, however, until the ethical (and legal) context is considered: where personal relationships in the workplace were long ignored, contextual ethics would suggest that the presence of a power imbalance, an exchange of money, or access to decision-making makes the matter one of concern for the board. If role ("protect the interests of shareholders, so it's our business") and personal morality ("relationships are private matters, so this is none of our business") come into conflict, alignment with the ethical context will ensure the best possible decision about the prospect of his removal ("Do the CEO's actions involve power, money, or access?").

Where there are gaps or differences among these three constructs is where the leader must make choices, and these choices will have consequences. Making everyone happy is impossible; the likelihood of the leader shaping a net-positive outcome is far greater than the likelihood of experiencing unmanageable blowback when the leader explores the moral, ethical, and role triangle in advance and as a matter of course.

Once that work has begun – and it is never finished, as it has to be refreshed regularly – leaders can make more intentional and explicit decisions that align with their values and enable them to operate with integrity.

Accordingly, the CEO grappling with the morality of laying off employees during an economic downturn might first clarify her desire to be experienced as both savvy and compassionate, her belief that business exists to generate wealth for individuals and communities, her view that the purpose of her specific business is to improve individuals' quality of life, and her understanding that fulfilling these purposes and beliefs requires the business to sustain itself profitably for the long run. She can then reconcile her view of the potential immorality of taking away livelihood during a period of economic challenge by noting the alignment of contextual ethics (that is, it is appropriate, ethical, and imperative to do what is necessary to sustain the company for the long-run) and her role (in other words, the needs of her total stakeholders – including the vast majority of employees – likely override the needs of any one individual).

The CEO who has communicated the desire to be both compassionate and savvy will recognize that some previous situations may have asserted one characteristic over the other. Before making the decision to reduce headcount, she can consider, "Where have previous decisions reflected my morals, ethical context, and role responsibilities congruently?" and "What's similar or different this time?" The outcome of this reflection might lead the CEO to a different decision – but it might instead lead to a reckoning between her underlying values and her communicated messaging.

Exploring how she has communicated what matters to her as a person, as a leader, and as a steward of the company – and how her previous actions have reinforced or undermined these messages – will help the CEO to understand the alignment and/or gap between her intent and her impact. She will then be able to look at seemingly conflictual decisions like layoffs with clarity: what do I want to stand for, what will my action suggest I genuinely stand for, and am I okay with a discrepancy there? Will my stakeholders be okay with that discrepancy? And if not, do I need to adjust my decision(s) or my ostensible values?

Making complex decisions under the pressure of time is a requirement of most leaders, but these decisions do not exist in a vacuum. The more each leader invests in exploring the integrity of her decision-making framework in the abstract, the better she can make tough calls quickly in the future. And each of these decisions will enable the leader to further sharpen her understanding of her underlying values, the role that she is fulfilling, the ethical context in which she is operating, and alignment or disparity among these – just in time for the next set of difficult choices.

In situations as deeply personal, truly complex, and with real human consequences as taking away an individual's employment (or others described above), nuance does not work to the leader's advantage. She must consider: what do I stand for most critically and clearly? And if that stand is clear, will others understand my decision without extensive, detailed explanation?

Difficult Decision: Containing Contagion

As the coronavirus outbreak continues, many multinational employers are rethinking how employees even outside of mainland China work

(Continued)

together, one chief executive says. Eric Pliner, CEO of YSC Consulting . . . tells WSJ that workers . . . throughout Asia find themselves cancelling air travel due to concerns about the virus. "Everyone is thinking about coronavirus right now," Pliner says . . . As a result, Pliner says many employers are now asking the same question: "How do we work globally if we have to reduce dependence on air travel?"
    – Chip Cutter, *Wall Street Journal*, 2020[7]

Six weeks after I gave this utterly scintillating interview, my own leadership team was still thinking about coronavirus but no longer limiting our debate to questions of travel. In truth, it wasn't a terribly difficult decision to close our largest offices the first time around. We'd considered our options from many angles, but the actual choice was reasonably straightforward. With a former employee comatose in one of the world's most highly publicized and prominent cases of what would eventually be known as long COVID, we understood all too well the stakes for individual well-being. The offices that had been affected by the novel coronavirus prior to March of 2020 were among our smallest, but they had taken swift action, arranged equipment and infrastructure to enable secure remote working, and successfully ensured reasonable comfort and support for employees working from home. Making the call to close hubs in London and New York, therefore, was made easier by test cases in less-populated markets but also by some

---

[7] Chip Cutter, "Auto & Transport Roundup: Market Talk." *Wall Street Journal, News Plus*. February 7, 2020.

degree of naïveté: We thought we'd be shutting down for a few weeks at most.

Because our moral obligation to care for the well-being of our people and their families aligned neatly with our ethical obligation to avoid putting people in harm's way and with only limited or short-term compromise to our responsibilities as leaders of a business, there was no notable conflict among the sides of the triangle. We were able to make an uncomfortable choice – to close the offices and ask everyone to work remotely for the short-term – without much real sacrifice.

Eighteen months later, as we prepared to reopen these same locations, our original questions took on different nuance, greater complexity, and an unexpected layer of conflict among the dimensions. We'd managed our role responsibilities to the business successfully, transferring our services from primarily in-person to primarily virtual, and there'd been limited change in our ethical context (we were still motivated by not wanting to put people in harm's way). But this time, there was a conflict between that ethical context, our responsibilities to our employees and customers to reopen our offices, and a critical moral belief held and enacted with reasonable consistency across our team: the belief in and support for autonomy and optionality regarding individual and family health choices.

For years, we'd offered a variety of flexible benefits that enabled employees to select the support that best matches their individual and/or family needs and budgets. The six weeks of annual leave that we granted to all employees was entirely flexible, and we strongly

(Continued)

encouraged its full use each year. We matched benefits to local market needs and demands, providing paid lunch options in some locations, extended a range of subsidized health plans in markets without government-sponsored medicine, provided a mix of paid and unpaid leave options (up to a year) for new parents, gave sabbaticals every four years to professional services staff, and offered all team members unrestricted leave for bereavement and for mental, physical, and other health needs. We made mistakes and adjustments along the way, but the bottom line underpinning our approach to our employees was to recognize individual humanity, foster personal choice, and to allow people to craft the path that was most right for them and their circumstances.

Further, two years prior, we'd introduced our entire firm to the concept of *community care*. In doing so, we worked to remove the selfishness implicit in self-care by upending the belief that individuals must do what they need to do for themselves regardless of the impact on others and replacing it instead with the belief that we all have the responsibility, obligation, and opportunity to care for ourselves while caring for each other. That shift in impact had been profound, resulting in colleagues making sure that they weren't dumping unfinished work on others when they went off on vacation, managing our communication styles and channels with greater attentiveness to individual preferences and needs, and even introducing "meet-free Fridays," a day to catch up on work without the burden of internal meetings and calls.

Although we didn't spot it in advance, the conflict between individual choice and community care seems glaringly obvious now. While some of our employees around the world clamored desperately for access to vaccines, several in the US insisted that COVID vaccination was a deeply personal choice that they'd elected to avoid – some for faith-based reasons, some for reasons of historical bias in medicine against Black Americans and other people of color, and some for personal health reasons, among others. At the same time, our team included employees with family members who could not be vaccinated (such as children under 12, for whom the vaccines were not yet approved) or who were immunocompromised (cancer survivors, those living with HIV/AIDS), and it had been established that vaccinated individuals could still carry the virus, making the notion of community care particularly important. And we weren't operating in isolation; we watched as President Biden "call[ed] on private companies to issue vaccine requirements"[8] and agonized as a subset of our employees begged for access to the office – partly as a component of their own quality of life.

We went back and forth among our lived moral belief (that it is right for individuals to be able to make the health choices that are most right for themselves and their loved ones, and that we as an employer should help to make that possible); our explicit ethical framework (that community care that includes self-care should always take precedence over pure self-care); and our role responsibilities (we had a business to run,

---

[8] Lauren Egan, "Biden Calls on Private Companies to Issue Vaccine Requirements," *NBC News*. August 23, 2021. https://www.nbcnews.com/politics/white-house/biden-calls-private-companies-issue-vaccine-requirements-n1277470.

investors to satisfy, and empty offices with fully paid rent on our books).

Ultimately, with congruence between our role responsibilities and ethical framework, the moral choice was clear. Or was it?

Key Points

- Leaders can and should design their desired leadership styles, interactions and dynamics, and organizational cultures with intent, rather than leaving these critical human elements to default.

- The most difficult decisions cannot be made objectively, no matter how many analytics we complete; they challenge us precisely because they are human and subjective.

- Personal morality, ethical context, and the role responsibilities of the leader all exist in service of good.

- Leadership is always interpersonal and affects real people's real lives.

- Every leadership decision contains both ethics and morals; understanding these clarifies the relationship between our individual beliefs and the expectations of our context.

- Making everyone happy is impossible; shaping a net-positive outcome is made more likely by exploring the moral, ethical, and role triangle regularly and in advance.

2

The Moral–Ethical–Role Responsibility Triangle

The most challenging decisions test us because they highlight disagreement or incongruence among people that really matter: ourselves, our key stakeholders, and the at-large organizations, societies, and/or cultures within which we operate and exist. Those three populations align to three lenses through which we can consider right and wrong, and those lenses form a triangle: the moral–ethical–role responsibilities triangle (Figure 2.1). Conflict within or among any side(s) of the triangle can be better understood and resolved by relying on the remaining dimensions.

Morals and ethics come into conflict when what we personally believe about what is right and what is wrong is ignored, disputed, or contradicted by what is considered acceptable in our organizations, societies, and cultures. Remember, morals are internally referenced, but they are

FIGURE 2.1 The Moral–Ethical–Role Responsibility Triangle

externally influenced. They don't just come out of nowhere, nor are they universally agreed. Ethics are externally referenced, but internally interpreted. They remind us that we exist in relationship to others.

For instance, someone who is vegan might believe that killing and consuming animals is immoral under any circumstance, but he is unlikely to encounter more than a few very limited contexts where that view is held by society or culture at large. (Although some ethicists do suggest that our collective view of the ethics of animal consumption is likely to change within our lifetimes.)[1] Still, if I believe that I cannot be comfortable in any place where animals are consumed, there are places in the world where I can reasonably construct an existence where I do not have to interact in animal-consuming environments.

But what if I am a leader of, for, and with other people? Can I avoid environments where others are consuming

---

[1]Melanie Joy, "Eating Meat Will Be Considered Unthinkable to Many 50 Years from Now," *Vox*, April 3, 2019, https://www.vox.com/2019/3/27/18174374/eating-meat-veganism-vegetarianism.

animals? Do I stay out of restaurants, avoid conferences, allow only vegan menus in the company cafeteria, prohibit others from bringing turkey sandwiches from home? How can I reconcile the boundaries of my personal morality with the fact that societal ethics generally consider some kinds of animal consumption to be acceptable?

Faced with this conflict, I can look to my role responsibilities to help me to determine how to proceed. Who do I serve? Who are my stakeholders? What do they want and need? What does my role in relation to other people tell me about how I can reconcile the gap between my personal morality and contextual ethics?

When my role requires me to engage in activities that are generally considered acceptable but that I personally believe to be wrong, the moral and role responsibilities dimensions of the triangle are in conflict. In those cases, I can use my morality to challenge my role responsibilities (a one-time proposition), or I can look to contextual ethics – what does the world at large have to say about what I am being asked to consider or do? – to help me to test the extent and depth of my morality.

What about when contextual ethics say that what my role responsibilities require is wrong or unnecessary? Perhaps a group of employees demand that I create a forum for talking about an upcoming election; my larger context – or even my board of directors – might suggest that a likely divisive, employer-sponsored discussion of politics at work is inappropriate or even unethical. As a leader, though, I have an obligation to serve my employees and to take their needs seriously. In such a case, I can look to my morality to tell me whether I personally believe that my employees' demands are reasonable and right or whether I'm being asked, in my role, to engage in activity that undermines the working experience of many stakeholders in response to the needs of a few.

What about when there isn't even alignment among my stakeholders? That is, when the dispute is among or within my role responsibilities? Even before personal morality or contextual ethics are on the table, how do I reconcile conflict among those I purport to serve? Understanding the needs and views of each stakeholder and then exploring these in light of morality and ethics help me to decide who best to serve, how, and when, and how to communicate with those who will believe that I am not serving their needs.

Every one of these dilemmas always contains a quit/leave option, but that's a card that most leaders get to play only once. Few stakeholders will tolerate a leader threatening to leave over every perceived moral or ethical dispute, especially because these conflicts arise for many leaders nearly every day. Absent complete social isolation (which negates the notion of leadership, as leadership is fundamentally an interpersonal and/or collaborative activity), we have to be able to navigate contradictions while still maintaining connections with other people. That takes moral absolutism off the table in all but the most extreme circumstances.

So the triangle is not merely a semantic framework; it is a profoundly practical one. While others have written far more eloquent treatises on notions of morality and ethics, and still others will in the future, I am interested in the intersection of three constructs that inform how we make decisions: what we believe at our core; what we understand to be acceptable in our current sociocultural or sociopolitical context; and what we commit to, explicitly or implicitly, by taking on a role – formally or informally – in an organization, a community, or even a family. When these align, decision-making is easy. When they do not – and for the most difficult challenges, they usually don't – our ability to understand each element on its own, and sort through their apparent conflict, is at the heart of whether we can made difficult decisions with skill, insight, and empathy.

The process of doing so isn't inherently easy. In fact, research has demonstrated that people with a weaker sense of morality[2] tend to have an easier time reconciling these high-stakes dilemmas, potentially helping to explain the prevalence of leaders with psychopathic tendencies.[3] But that's all the more reason to invest in understanding and cultivating your own starting point, ensuring that you are able to serve as a force for good in arenas rife with less-than-moral players.

We'll explore how to use the triangle in Chapter 6, after we look at each side in depth. For now, though, consider that when two sides come into conflict, we can look to the third to inform the best possible decision.

Morals versus Ethics: *Election*

In Alexander Payne's 1999 film *Election*, teacher Jim McAllister (played by Matthew Broderick) asks his high school government students to explain the difference between morals and ethics. They never do, exactly, although all of the characters spend most of the rest of the movie bringing both – or the absence of both – to life. The lesson leads McAllister to reflect on a conversation with his best friend, fellow teacher Dave Novotny (played by Mark Harelik). Novotny witlessly presents his sexual interactions with student Tracy Flick (played by Reese Witherspoon) as

[2] Benjamin R. Walker and Chris J. Jackson, "Moral emotions and corporate psychopathy: A review," *Journal of Business Ethics*, February 11, 2016, 797–810. https://link.springer.com/article/10.1007/s10551-016-3038-5.
[3] Karen Landay, P. D. Harms, and Marcus Crede, "Shall we serve the dark lords? A meta-analytic review of psychopathy and leadership," *Journal of Applied Psychology* 104(1), 2019, 183–196, https://www.apa.org/pubs/journals/features/apl-apl0000357.pdf.

those of star-crossed lovers: He is married, she is a high
school student with a mom who "doesn't understand."

Jim: Dave, I'm just saying this as your friend. What
          you're doing is really, really wrong, and you've
          gotta stop. The line you've crossed is immoral,
          and it's illegal.

Dave: Jim, come on. I don't need a lecture on ethics.

Jim: I'm not talking about ethics. I'm talking
          about morals.

Dave: *(a beat)* What's the difference?

Played for laughs, the scene is nonetheless chilling when
taken on its merits. Novotny has confessed to the statutory
rape of a 15-year-old who is under his supervision. The
question, as Jim suggests, is not whether our current social
context has elevated adolescents to adulthood, with the
ability to rationally consent to sexual relationships, nor is it
whether others might find some reason to deem the
relationship acceptable. These are ethical frames, Jim
intimates, and they are superseded by what is fundamentally
a moral question: Is it wrong for an adult with differentiated
power, earned or granted, fairly or unfairly, by virtue of age,
experience, cognitive sophistication, gender, role as an
authority figure, or otherwise to engage in a sexual
relationship with someone on the other side of every aspect
of that power equation?

Of course, the ethical context of the 1990s was different
from today. Four months prior to *Election*'s release, President
Bill Clinton was impeached for and ultimately acquitted of
charges of perjury for lying about a sexual relationship with
Monica Lewinsky, a White House intern in her early
twenties. Plenty of mainstream commentators across the
political spectrum painted Lewinsky as an aggressor who

seduced a popular president with a known pattern of abuses that had been largely dismissed as "indiscretions." Hindsight has shifted the focus of mainstream conversation about Lewinsky and Clinton from one of contextual ethics – heightened by the national narrative about workplace sexual harassment brought to bear by Dr. Anita Hill during Justice Clarence Thomas's 1991 Supreme Court confirmation hearings – to one of morality. That is, regardless of one's ability to consent, which Lewinsky clearly had, was Clinton's participation in and/or pursuit of a sexual relationship with Lewinsky amidst a clear gap in the power and authority assigned to their respective roles just plain wrong?

It is perhaps of note that *Election*, with its Ross Perot-esque spoiler candidate and conflation of morals, ethics, and role responsibilities, is often described as an allegory for the 1992 US presidential election that first put Clinton in federal office. And Flick's bold ambition as a female candidate for school president has made her an obvious if unfortunate referent for another Clinton. In 2015, Reese Witherspoon told attendees at a Producers Guild conference, "When I did meet Hillary Clinton, she said, 'Everybody talks to me about Tracy Flick in *Election*.'"[4]

Jean and Paula

If morals and ethics are both essentially frameworks for separating good from bad or right from wrong, does the distinction between them really matter so much?

---

[4]See Dave McNary, "Reese Witherspoon on Portraying Hillary Clinton, Finding Great Roles for Women," *Variety*, May 30, 2015, https://variety.com/2015/film/news/reese-witherspoon-hillary-clinton-tracy-flick-produced-by-1201508768/, and Megan Garber, "Hillary Clinton, Tracy Flick, and the Reclaiming of Female Ambition," *The Atlantic*, June 9, 2016. https://www.theatlantic.com/entertainment/archive/2016/06/hillary-clinton-tracy-flick-and-the-reclaiming-of-ambition/486389/.

Considering the delicate subtlety in their differences and the seeming casualness with which people swap them for each other, the frequency with which morals and ethics conflict is perhaps surprising. It is easy to dismiss Inspector Javert from *Les Misérables* as heartless for his lifelong pursuit of retribution for Jean Valjean's theft of bread to feed his children and his subsequent escape from his assigned punishment of hard labor. Perhaps Javert is behaving ethically ("thou shalt not steal") while Valjean behaves morally, preventing his starving children from greater suffering. However, as we read *Les Misérables* (okay, fine, watch the musical) we are clearly guided to have greater empathy for its moral protagonist, and not only when his foil is enacted feebly by Russell Crowe. Ethics are essential, we are left to believe, except when they are superseded by morals.

But this is not always the case. In one plotline among many in auteur Mike White's miniseries *The White Lotus*, college sophomore Paula (Brittany O'Grady) tags along with her friend Olivia (Sydney Sweeney) and family on a trip to the eponymous hotel, an isolated Hawaiian paradise catering to wealthy and mostly white mainlanders.[5] As the only person of color in her party of five – and a horny teenager to boot – Paula quickly finds connection with native Hawaiian hotel employee Kai (Kekoa Scott Kekumano), who explains the theft of family land by the government, its subsequent sale to the developers of the hotel, and the profound economic impact of these activities on his family and community.

---

[5]James Poniewozik, "Review: 'The White Lotus' Offers Scenery from the Class Struggle," *The New York Times*, July 8, 2021, https://www.nytimes.com/2021/07/08/arts/television/review-white-lotus.html.

Enamored of her vacation romance, angered by his tragic story, and disillusioned by her hosts, whose values she ostensibly rejects, Paula concocts what she foolishly perceives as a simple, elegant transfer of wealth. She recognizes that her plan is both illegal and unethical (hence her reluctance to get her own hands dirty) but essentially rationalizes it with a straightforward moral argument: They stole more, they stole first, and their theft created greater harm.

I don't intend to spoil the story here; you've had a century and a half to read *Les Misérables* and far less time to watch *The White Lotus*. But even if she is right in her moral certitude, when Paula's plan goes awry, it is patently obvious that morals are essential – except, perhaps, when they are superseded by ethics.

Sigh.

Stolen bread or stolen land? Hungry family or . . . hungry family? It's not clear. With so much conflict between them, we cannot, apparently, expect to consistently side with both morals and ethics simultaneously. And there is no simple way to give one obvious preference over the other.

Absolutism isn't going to work. We can't expect to make difficult decisions or to filter our understanding of situational complexity by purporting to align ourselves to either morality or ethics – or by twisting ourselves into knots attempting to align to both. That doesn't make us immoral or unethical, but it does mean that the ability to make informed and compassionate choices with any sort of consistency and integrity – knowing that every choice involves a trade-off – depends on meaningful understanding of the sources of our morality and the context for our ethical frameworks.

The more we explore our own decision-making frameworks in the abstract, the better equipped we will be to make tough calls when the job requires it. (The arts and entertainment make for particularly helpful ways to do that abstract exploration, which is among the reasons you will see those channels for storytelling referenced throughout this text.) Each of these elements will help to further sharpen your understanding of your underlying morals, the role that you are fulfilling, and the ethical context in which you are operating – just in time to make your next difficult choice.

Win as Much as You Can

The simulation exercise "Win as Much as You Can" (WAMAYC) has become a staple of negotiation programs, business school curricula, and social justice training. Drawn from the prisoner's dilemma, a fundamental tenet of game theory, WAMAYC allows participants to explore principles of cooperation, collaboration, competition, and reward. Versions of the prisoner's dilemma show up in gameshows like the UK's *Golden Balls*, the US's *Friend or Foe?*; "reality" shows like *Love Island*, *The Challenge*, and *FBoy Island* (yep, that's real); and even films like *The Warriors* and the *Saw* franchise. The basic conundrum is almost always the same: Do I influence, deceive, or abandon you in the hope of getting a bigger or better positive outcome for myself or my team, or do I collaborate with you to get a solid result for all of us – knowing full well that I might end up with nothing or be otherwise harmed if you've influenced, deceived, or abandoned me in return?

In WAMAYC, teams move quickly through a series of rounds where they make a simple choice: X or Y. If all of the participating teams choose X, they share a pot of points. If any one of the participating teams chooses Y while at least one other chooses X, the teams that choose Y share in the reward, while the teams that choose X get nothing. Communication across the teams is only allowed after select rounds, and some rounds offer bonus points. Once the exercise has begun, facilitators can repeat only one instruction: "Win as much as you can."

I first encountered this exercise 30 years ago under the tutelage of educator Cheryl Hollman Keen and leadership expert Jim Keen, who used it to introduce concepts of joint gains, trust, and community to groups of ambitious, socially minded adolescents; I've used it in lots of settings since, as recently as six months ago with the executive team of a Fortune 500 company (nearly all of whom had completed it at least once before – and therefore knew the rules and possible outcomes). And despite dozens of implementations across contexts, sectors, demographic groups, industries, and geographies for almost three decades, I have never witnessed a group decide consistently to collaborate in the face of opportunity to compete – even when its participants know the game well already.

I have no particular judgment of that outcome; after all, the game is called "Win as Much as You Can." Its lessons – and there are many – depend in part on individual and collective interpretation of the words in the title. What does it mean to "win"? What is "as much as you can"? And who is "you"?

Those questions align to the sides of the triangle:

- **What does it mean to "win"?** How does the way that we win affect our experience or interpretation of winning? What do I believe about winning? Does someone have to lose for someone else to win? How do our answers to these questions shed light on our own morality – or what we think "right" and "wrong" mean?

- **What is "as much as you can"?** Am I looking to gain the most for myself and my stakeholders? What choices will generally be seen as acceptable and experienced as positive in the context that we're completing the exercise? What do my interpretations of those collective expectations tell me about my context and the ethics that inform it?

- **Who is "you"?** In my role, to and for whom am I responsible? For whom do I work? Who are my stakeholders? And how does my view of my role responsibilities change based on my view of my stakeholders?

How we answer these questions gives us some clues not only about how we can define and achieve success in this exercise – but how we can make the difficult decisions that allow us to define and achieve success as leaders.

Difficult Decision: Furloughing 80 Percent of the Ralph Lauren Workforce

Smack in the center of the Ralph Lauren Corporation's corporate page, offset by a dashing photo of Mr. Lauren plus several models draped in the brand's distinctive styles, is the company's purpose statement: "Our enduring purpose, that guides everything we do, is to inspire the dream of a better life through authenticity and timeless style." When the COVID-19 public health and economic crises of 2020 hit this fifty-four-year-old Fortune 500 company hard – as it did so many retailers – President and Chief Executive Officer Patrice Louvet kept returning to that single, powerful sentence. In the role of CEO not even three years (after a successful career at Procter & Gamble), Louvet was suddenly confronted by a massive challenge, the likes of which neither he nor the company had previously encountered.[6]

"COVID was spreading around the world, stores were closing, consumers were staying home, teams were worried about going to work, and as a result of all of that, revenue was plummeting," Louvet explains. At the time, "Only e-commerce was operating, and even that was shutting down, as infections began to spread within our distribution centers. And we had to preserve cash. We're asking ourselves, is this going to last a few weeks? Months? Ten years? Cash is [critical]; we're thinking about how we preserve cash for as long as possible in order to sustain beyond the pandemic. [It felt like] the business was disappearing overnight."

"Of course, we want the company to be vibrant for at least another fifty years and more," Louvet says, "But that was at risk. If it ever went down, 24,000 jobs would disappear, and that has impact on all of our employees and their families and all of the communities that we serve and support."

(Continued)

[6]All quotes from Patrice Louvet in this chapter are from an interview with Eric Pliner, September 2021.

To understand the scope of the challenge, Louvet and team first "pored over data for endless hours to think about how to achieve consistency and fairness. We had to protect our cash position and aggressively manage expenses. We did an exercise to layout the key areas of cash burn. We had to look at management of inventory, of rent. In many instances, we had to renegotiate our rents. We froze all open hires, we stopped freelance and consulting work, stopped all capital investments, all real estate buildouts. We looked at every line of cash utilization and took tough steps across all of it."

And still, it wasn't enough. "The situation was dire. We needed to take even more meaningful interventions." But the next big area of cash outlay was people, which the team had been reluctant to consider. "We came to the conclusion that we had to do something in this space. But if we were going to even consider that possibility, we had to [be able to] tell the organization, 'This is a carefully considered decision, we've turned over every stone, we need to do it for the long-term viability of the company.'"

And so, in what was "one of the most difficult decisions we ever had to make as a leadership team and undoubtedly the hardest I have ever had to make as a CEO," Louvet says, "we had to determine whether to furlough the majority of the company workforce to preserve cash during the COVID shutdown."

"We went to our purpose and our principles to help us navigate the situation," Louvet recalls. "Our thinking was, this is going to cause serious pain for people, and people are the heart of the company. But in light of our purpose, my role as the CEO is to protect the long-term viability of the enterprise so we can continue to inspire the dream of a better life for all of our stakeholders."

"We looked at all of it through the lenses of different stakeholders. It was a multistakeholder moment. It wasn't just Ralph or the board or investors. We had to weigh everything through the perspectives of lots of different people to come to the best decision possible. Obviously, Ralph – as the founder and as the holder of the company values and the company purpose – cares so deeply about the long-term viability of what he's built. He was very supportive very quickly. He cares so much about our people and the team that he's built over time but understood that we needed to do this. Next, was the executive leadership team and the global leadership team. We had a lot of discussion – how long would we do this? Where? When? Then it was about explaining the decision to a larger leadership group, enrolling the leaders so they understood what we were doing before we went to the broader organization. Our investors obviously care about the viability of their investment in our company."

All of those stakeholder groups were obvious, but they were only a starting point. "We immediately thought through the people impacted and what this would mean for them. There wasn't a clear right or wrong. It was uncharted territory – the whole situation was. There was no playbook to refer to. We

(Continued)

really tried to look at how we try to minimize the trade-offs and the pain. We thought through our consumers – what would they say [when they became] aware of this? What would this say about the brand and the company? Would they say we were living our purpose, or would they say that we were working against the values and purpose that we'd built for years? What would it mean for our communities and partners? If you look at how many people we employ directly and indirectly – it's millions. We have more than 20,000 employees directly, but we impact the livelihoods of millions of people and families around the world. We're a top supplier to other businesses and our deterioration would've been a major blow to them and their employees and their communities, too."

"We debated the perspectives and the interests of all of the stakeholders," Louvet continues. "People understood the severity of the situation quickly, what this meant if we did it and if we did not."

In the end, Louvet and team made the choice that they "believed was most responsible, [in service of] the long-term health of the company. We furloughed 80 percent of our workforce."

He continues, "We did other things in parallel, of course – we allocated foundation funds to support employees, we created an Employee Relief Fund that supported our colleagues who were facing medical, eldercare or childcare needs. We did tap into our own resources and government programs, to support anyone affected. For example, we made available grants for any eligible employee who applied and leveraged government programs where we could in order to complement revenue for some employees. Management took pay cuts, the board cut its fees, Ralph gave up a year of compensation, I gave up 50 percent of my compensation, the Global Leadership Team gave up 25 percent of its compensation."

If the choice itself wasn't hard enough, figuring out how best to communicate the decision presented a whole new set of challenges.

"I did a video from my home," Louvet recalls. "I framed out why we were doing this. We spent a lot of time on why – clearly and consistently. And I had a real need to demonstrate empathy, to do it as authentically and genuinely as possible."

Even so, Louvet says, "We knew not everyone would agree. We knew we couldn't make the pain go away, but we wanted people to understand the drivers of the decision. The decision required us to make difficult choices now, to rebound quickly, to be a strong industry leader and the employer we have always been. We were focused on being agile and proactive to ensure we were positioned to come back strong. We put a lot of emphasis on hope. We needed to instill hope in our people, in addition to holding the hope for the company."

That focus on hope wasn't without balance. "We recognized the pain that the decisions would cause people," Louvet says. "We also knew that these actions made us stronger in the long run. Had we not done it, the company could've depleted, which would've been

(Continued)

permanently devastating for our employees, devastating for our communities, for our founder, for our investors, for the consumers who love this brand and for whom it plays a role in their life."

To the surprise of the business' leaders, the decision was well received overall. "Most people understood. They appreciated the transparency, the thought process, the thinking behind it and the support we were offering. They got it, and they knew they'd work through it. That doesn't minimize the pain, and no doubt it doesn't represent the view of everyone impacted, but it was powerful. I was really inspired by that response. There was no massive backlash, none of that. People understood what needed to be done, which says a lot about the organization. Ultimately, people knew that we wouldn't make this decision if we weren't living what really mattered to us as a company."

And perhaps even more incredibly, "About 70 percent of the furloughed people came back. People felt a degree of loyalty and commitment to the company, even after the furlough. Many of these people are eminently employable in the market. But they came back to us. That really says something."

"The power of going back to our purpose was extraordinary," Louvet reflects. "It was a real guide. It helped corral us and get everyone aligned. I look back at this and I think it was one of the toughest and ultimately one of the most courageous leadership decisions I had to make in my life."

He goes on: "I understood that it was what we had to do, but I felt horrible about this decision. It was close to 20,000 people. It put lots of people in a very difficult situation. We tried to help them as best as we could. But we had to make the decision based on what matters to us, the values and our purpose. I don't mean to minimize the impact. It created real hardship for people. We did not make this choice lightly. We'd twisted it in every way we could to figure something out. Given the world, given the uncertainty, it was what we needed to do."

Do the Right Thing

Are the tough decisions that we face as leaders really difficult enough to warrant all of this process? Can't we just hold ourselves and others to a simple standard – "do the right thing" – and save the hours of introspection that the exercises on the following pages seem to demand?

Maybe. The truth is that we never really know if whatever choices we've made were, in fact, the right ones. We can spend hours after the fact rationalizing with relief why we've done what was best for everyone involved, but that's more about soothing our own anxieties and fears than it is about asserting any sort of factual accuracy. We never really know what might've resulted from another choice. When Robert Frost writes that he "took the [road] less traveled by / and that has made all the difference,"[7] he doesn't actually have any idea if that's the case; he's just reassuring himself in ABAAB rhyme scheme.

---

[7] Robert Frost, "The Road Not Taken," 1915, The Poetry Foundation, https://www. poetryfoundation.org/poems/44272/the-road-not-taken.

Our definitions of what exactly constitutes "the right thing" vary dramatically – and what is right for us as individuals may not match with what is right for the people and organizations that we lead or the societies and cultures within which we lead them. We have to know what we mean by "right," what conditions might alter that definition, and how we hope to be able to communicate about where we're coming from.

Key Points

- Morals and ethics conflict when our personal beliefs about right and wrong are ignored, disputed, or contradicted by what is considered acceptable in our organizations, societies, and cultures.

- Morals are internally referenced, but they are externally influenced. They don't just come out of nowhere, nor are they universally agreed.

- Ethics are externally referenced, but internally interpreted. They remind us that we exist in relationship to other people.

- Leaders have to navigate contradictions while still maintaining connections with other people. That demands negotiation, which leaves absolutism off the table in all but the most extreme circumstances.

- It's not enough to hope to "do the right thing"; the more we explore our own decision-making frameworks in the abstract, the better equipped we are to serve as forces for good when confronted with difficult, real decisions.

3

Morals

Want to see a whole room go silent? Ask people to talk about morality – especially their own morality.

When I opened the floor for questions during an early presentation of the moral–ethical–role responsibility triangle, an audience member pounced instantly. "I'm really uncomfortable with the idea of morality," she said, "and I don't think I'm alone in that. Can we use the word *values* instead? That seems more relevant to me."

There is certainly a place for values in discussion of decision-making. Knowing what's important to us and what we prioritize in making decisions, organizing our lives, and building our relationships is clearly relevant – and it's also a heck of a lot more comfortable. Values are interesting and convey plenty about what matters to each of us, but they're also subject to careful curation and the pressure of social desirability. Is this stuff what really matters to me, or does it make me look and feel good to say that these are my values?

Morals are the inverse. They represent a bottom line, often drawn in thick, black Sharpie (at first, anyway). They are, at their core and ours, about what we deem to be right and wrong. Morals escape the flowery language and narrative massage of values statements, even when they are aligned. Values tell us what we stand for – but morals tell us what we absolutely *won't* stand for.

Lots of people are uncomfortable with the idea of morality as a component of leadership. There's plenty of good reason to be cautious about the notion and language of morality. Throughout the 1980s, in the United States, the "Moral Majority" referred to a right-wing, faith-connected organization led by American preacher Jerry Falwell. From the perspectives of voter turnout, financial support, and narrative control, the Moral Majority was wildly successful. The organization's activities played a critical role in three consecutive American presidential election cycles and countless local votes in between. It also shifted popular discourse about the notion of morality. Those aligned to its views, the Moral Majority platform intimated, were moral. Those misaligned, including feminists, those opposed to religious prayer in public schools, those supporting abortion access, and gay and lesbian people (before bisexual, transgender, and other queer identities were acknowledged or taken seriously) were either without an understanding of right and wrong (amoral) or behaving in ways that they knew were wrong (immoral).

The Moral Majority's cultural dominance allowed for a popular misconception to fester. There is not, despite the organization's successful campaign to the contrary, a single morality. We can, do, and must coexist with different notions of what is right and what is wrong. Absent social acceptability of open discussion of what morals mean to each of us, though, it is all too easy for a single, extreme paradigm to set the terms of collective understanding of – and for all of us to blindly position ourselves in relation to – that understanding.

The notion that right and wrong are not absolutes can be a difficult pill to swallow. Pressed to identify a baseline, personal, non-negotiable moral, we might easily defer to the simple idea that humans should not kill other humans. Easy enough; most major world religions include some version of this tenet: Sikhism, Jainism, and Buddhism outright prohibit killing or harming any living thing; Hinduism rejects killing, violence, and revenge; "no killing" is the first precept of Taoism; Islam considers killing a human being without just cause a major sin; and Judaism and Christianity include "Thou Shalt Not Kill" among the Decalogue or Ten Commandments (albeit with some caveats to this proclamation in other texts of the three Abrahamic religions). While religion is not, as we have noted, our only source of morality, it is nonetheless a major influence and a reasonable proxy for understanding aspects of morality formation.

Seems pretty straightforward: Don't kill anyone. But how clear, exactly, is this baseline of morality? Are we adequately moral if we do not directly cause an individual's death? What if we are directly responsible for creating conditions that lead to deaths, no matter how inadvertently? Some years ago, I worked with leaders at a South African mining company whose grounds were dotted with signs identifying for employees and visitors the number of injury-free days and fatality-free shifts in as matter-of-fact a manner as if they were counting billions of burgers sold. Should the company's basic morality – and license to operate – be called into question every time the number resets? Do the end users of the products made from minerals mined by this company even ask these questions? Do they even think to do so?

And what of those billions of burgers – and their associated health consequences? What if we are indirectly responsible for deaths, by creating conditions or participating in systems or working for organizations whose products and services are known contributors to the loss of human life? What of our blood diamonds and smart phones and lithium batteries?

Maybe, as Oprah Winfrey indicated that Maya Angelou once told her, "When you know better, you do better."[1]

But what if, after Leonardo DiCaprio movies and SkyNews exposés and Morgan Spurlock documentaries, we know differently about the environment but we do nothing differently? Are we then without morality?

I don't think so. But we probably haven't spent much time clarifying our morality and its sources, either. Philosophers and religious scholars and psychologists – not to mention artists and politicians – have had plenty to say about these questions, and my reflections add little to their answers. At one end of the spectrum, moral absolutists shame those who suggest that these questions yield far more gray than black or white; at the other end, moral relativists risk substituting rationalization for genuine morality.

Leaders needn't align to one or the other, nor must they defend either. But it is incumbent upon each of us with desire or responsibility to lead others to understand what we think "right" and "wrong" are really about, to investigate the sources of these ideas, and to be prepared to talk about them with clarity, calm, curiosity, courage, and connection.

[1] Oprah Winfrey, "The Powerful Lesson Maya Angelou Taught Oprah," *Oprah's Life Class*, October 19, 2011, https://www.oprah.com/oprahs-lifeclass/the-powerful-lesson-maya-angelou-taught-oprah-video.

Understanding our own morality and using it to drive great decision-making demands a uniquely vulnerable mindset that requires acceptance of our fallibility. It requires us to acknowledge that morality itself is asymptotic – a curve that approaches but never actually meets a line of genuine good. This is why discussion of values is much easier than discussion of morals, and why interrogating and exploring our own morality is so essential for all of us – especially leaders.

Communicating Your Morality and Asking about Morality

Consider the following statement, made by a world leader: *I think I am a great moral leader.*

This statement tells us little about the nature or quality of the speaker's leadership, nor does it tell us much about the nature or quality of the individual's morality. But what it does tell us is that the speaker believes that he applies his understanding of morality to his leadership, and is confident that he does so successfully.

Without knowing anything else about the speaker, I am inclined to agree.

As I regularly tell the executives who I coach, my own team, and even my children, each of us is the hero of our own story. With very few exceptions, no one believes that they are the villain. If you have an adversarial relationship with someone else whose morality, decision-making, values, or way of engaging in the world (or just engaging with you) you consider to be problematic or wrong, odds are good that said individual feels the same about you in return. They don't see themselves as wreaking havoc on (insert your name here) City; they see themselves with an "S" on their chest, fighting the forces of evil that emanate from your dark lair. Few people would describe themselves as immoral or amoral – but our respective views of morality may not align.

So when someone says that they think they are a great moral leader, I think they're telling the truth – they *do* believe in their own moral greatness. I might not agree with that conclusion, but most of us do believe that our morality is right; otherwise, we'd change it. That's why it's so important for every leader to learn how to communicate the contents of our moral code clearly and appropriately.

In this case, the speaker who thought he was a great moral leader was the 45th president of the United States, Donald Trump. It taxes the imagination very little to entertain the notion that many people reacted with derision; actor-comedian Patton Oswalt tweeted sarcastically, "I think I have six-pack abs" in response, while actor-comedian Julia Louis-Dreyfus responded, "I think I can breathe underwater with my gills."[2] Point taken: Just because I think it doesn't make it true.

But it's not that Donald Trump is wrong in thinking that he's a great moral leader; it's that others either do not know, do not understand, do not agree with, or do not share his view of morality or moral leadership. I am perhaps more cautious about whether the former president has done the reflection to consider the sources of his morality and shape his use of it with intent; but that doesn't mean he is leading without morals. They just might not be universally shared morals.

It is not our job to influence each other's morality – and it's unlikely that we'd be successful. Longstanding research

[2] Hoffman, A., "Trump Said 'I Think I Am a Great Moral Leader' and the Internet Took It from There," *Time*, 7 November 2018. https://time.com/5448224/trump-moral-leader-jokes/

into children's moral development suggests that the foundations for independent moral thinking are typically in place by age 10, continuing evolution through adolescence into early adulthood.[3] Notable problems with this research notwithstanding (e.g., the small, single-gender sample size; alignment to Western cultural norms; use of an imaginary and/or inauthentic assessment; a model that is strictly linear rather than situationally applied),[4] adults, in general, do not waver dramatically in our interpretation of parameters of moral right and wrong. We might move at the margins, but our fundamentals stay reasonably consistent. All of those examples that you're thinking of right now – built via all-night college conversations or substance-related awakenings of awareness or study-abroad semesters or life-changing moments in hospital corridors – I would argue that these are shifts in our understanding or awareness of how morality is applied, not in the true underlying morals themselves.

It is perfectly reasonable for leaders to attempt to influence the application of morality in their leadership contexts – so long as we do so with proactive transparency, integrity, insight, and empathy. Proactive transparency requires open, clear communication about what you stand for as a leader and what you will not stand for, and that's hard.

After all, knowing that you're unlikely to shift another's view to align to your own, that morality is intimate and often private, and that discrimination on the basis of some of the known core influences on morality development (like religion, national origin, sex/gender) is illegal in many

---

[3] See Jean Piaget, Ved Varma, and Phillip Williams, *Piaget, Psychology and Education: Papers in Honour of Jean Piaget* (London: Hodder and Stoughton, 1976) and Lawrence Kohlberg, *Essays on Moral Development, Vol. I: The Philosophy of Moral Development* (San Francisco: Harper & Row, 1981).

[4] Martha Lally and Suzanne Valentine-French, "Kohlberg's Stages of Moral Development," *Lifespan Development, A Psychological Perspective* (Libre Texts: 2019).

nations around the world, why would any leader ever take on the risk associated with communicating a personal view of morality?

Well, you might not. On the one hand, communication of morality does not, in and of itself, imply an act of discrimination or an expectation of alignment to one's own moral view. Communicated without skill, however, explicit moral expression risks creating environments that those with divergent views experience as silencing or alienating. That's not great for enabling an inclusive, motivated populace, and it can be a source of perceived disparate treatment.

But in leadership contexts that foster genuine curiosity and authentic interpersonal connection, the demonstration of courage and vulnerability that accompanies discussion of one's own experiences and moral views can be a powerful tool for engaging a range of stakeholders in great decision-making. Even when your people don't agree, knowing and understanding where you're coming from and why helps others to align more quickly to your leadership choices.

Now, the operative word above is *skill*, so before you start making a mess by spouting your morality all over the place, let's consider instead how to begin to build skill in three areas: knowing the sources of your morality, understanding its true underlying parameters and boundaries, and determining what is directly relevant to your leadership context.

And, hey – you, too, might be a great moral leader. You probably already think you are.

Triangle Touchpoint: Values Conflict

Is it unethical to accept a role, especially a leadership role, knowing that your personal morality conflicts with the values and morals of the hiring organization?

Probably, but how are you supposed to know the values and morals of the hiring organization?

Let's start with the "probably." Assuming you are clear on your own morals and values (you likely aren't, at least not yet!), accepting a role where you know that what the organization stands for – and will not stand for – conflicts with your own ideology represents a kind of fraud. As employees (especially leaders), individuals represent the organizations that employ them and likely have an ethical obligation to be able to stand for those publicly.

But there are lots of assumptions implied in that answer. Certainly, the degree of ethical obligation likely increases the more senior the role. Alignment at every level of an organization might be deeply desirable, but it's far more reasonable to expect more from the C-suite than from front-line service employees. (That said, where organizations often fall off with another key stakeholder group – customers – is with those front-line workers, suggesting that organization-wide buy-in is more essential than may seem readily apparent.) The size of the gap between the individual and the organization and the scope of opportunity for influence might be another consideration; if I'm being hired into a role where I can shape the organization's approach to

(Continued)

morality, I might be more inclined to take on an opportunity with initial misalignment.

Anyway, individual opportunities can't be examined entirely out of context; the availability or scarcity of relevant jobs, the degree to which the individual needs employment, the comparability of compensation across employers, and the hiring practices of various prospective employers are all significant factors, too, among others. Access and opportunity play a critical component in whether any of us has the luxury of turning down work. In the abstract, though, it's fair to say that accepting a role with known misalignment in morals is certainly less than ideal, and is potentially unethical.

Where things get tricky, though, is that it's not the place or even the right of the organization to make that determination. That's up to the individual. It is illegal in many places for an employer to ask a candidate about the components of identity or experience that contribute to the individual's moral compass. Therefore, it is incumbent upon the organization to communicate its values and morals – what you will and won't stand for as an organization – so that the individual can make an educated determination.

It may not be okay for an interviewer to inquire about the candidate's morality, but I would argue that it is profoundly ethical – essential, even – for an employer to convey the organization's moral code up front.

If you're an organizational leader, you're probably an interviewer more frequently than you're a candidate. Consider, therefore, what everyone in a hiring scenario can do to ensure that the difficult decision about hiring for a role and the parallel difficult decision about pursuing and accepting a role are completed with the utmost integrity.

When you are a leader, work with colleagues and other senior leaders to ensure that you've revisited and refreshed your statement of values – and also talked openly about the organization's moral principles. As you consider what you stand for, what you won't stand for, and what you believe, work together to imagine the scenarios that disprove the statement. What happens if you are in extreme circumstances? How does your shared morality look if your ethical context changes? Where do you absolutely draw the line, and where is it fuzzier?

Next, consider what you want to tell others about what you've determined. Is there a succinct way to encapsulate your point of view? How can you share it with employees? Candidates? Customers? Does it go on your website? In your offices (if you have them)? How often do you reconsider and refresh what you've written and shared so that it's more accurate, less wrong, and more continually evolving in service of representing what really matters?

When you are a candidate, start with yourself. Spend some time considering the sources of your morality and your values. What do (you believe) you stand for personally? As a professional? What will you refuse to stand for? What do you feel confident that you can proclaim from a street corner or in the press or online for eternal record on behalf of your new

(Continued)

employer? What will you absolutely not stand behind if you were to be questioned or challenged publicly – or privately by a close friend or family member?

Next, do your research on the organization. They'll be doing due diligence on you, so do the same in return. Consider a mix of internal and external referencing. Ask what they say on paper about their values (often as easy as downloading a statement) and morals (probably nothing codified) and ask about how these are lived in practice. Look for alignment and/or differences among different stakeholder groups: What do other leaders say? Board members? Current employees? Former employees?

Your ability to determine whether there is alignment between your personal morality, the organization's ethical context, and the responsibilities of the role that you're considering depends upon how well you can triangulate – yes, triangulate – data across these three dimensions.

Knowing the Sources of Your Morality

Remember: Morals don't just come out of nowhere. They are internally referenced, but they are externally influenced. We aren't born with developed morality, but instead assume views and identities as informed by a variety of sources throughout our lives – starting with our parents or other primary caregivers, continuing through informal and formal education (secular, religious, or otherwise), incorporating media and art and literature,[5] and so on.

---

[5] Paula M. L. Moya, "Does Reading Literature Make You More Moral?," *Boston Review*, February 24, 2014. http://bostonreview.net/blog/paula-ml-moya-does-reading-literature-make-you-more-moral.

Religion is a big influence on our understanding of right and wrong – even where we don't identify with a particular religious doctrine. Entire societies are organized around dominant faith codes, many of which we internalize from early ages – regardless of whether we adopt these faith-based principles as our own. Other inputs to our respective internal views of right and wrong include cultural identity, personal and family experiences, individual psychology, the extent of our exposures to a variety of perspectives, crucible moments in our lives, and beyond.

Knowing, understanding, and holding intentional awareness of the source of our moral core is essential to making decisions with consistency and integrity. Contrary to stereotypes of morality, developing such self-awareness is not about locating an unmalleable central truth. It is instead about acknowledging what we think (and what we think we think!) and why, recognizing that true self-knowledge is ever evolving. It's also about aligning our behaviors to our beliefs.

Reflecting on the Sources of Your Morality

Think back to your early adolescence, around the age of thirteen or so. What do you remember most vividly? What were you most drawn to academically, socially, physically, and in your world? What made you most uncomfortable?

Who did you look to for guidance about how to grow and evolve yourself? Who were your role models and influences? What did you learn from each of these people? Whose approval did you seek? Peers? Teachers? Parents? Clergy? Activity leaders? Siblings? Strangers? Someone else? No one?

What moments and memories are most salient for you? What do those moments tell you about who you were, and what do those memories tell you about who you are today?

How are you still like the person that you were at thirteen? How are you different? What messages would you want to deliver to that kid if you could meet up now? What would that kid think of your career today? Of your priorities?

Depending on your degree of self-awareness, understanding influences on your worldview and development at critical times of life can help you to know more about how you crafted and embodied your moral code.

Understanding the Parameters and Boundaries of Your Morality

A lot of this sounds theoretical, and we want to know how to draw on morality very practically to answer difficult questions.

In principle, most of our daily decisions align with our morals. We generally behave in ways that reflect what we believe, how we want to live in the world, and how we want others to experience us or think of us. Where our actions and our beliefs don't align, it's probably because we have erroneously miscalculated our sense of self by replacing who we really are with who we want to be. Morality is like air entering and exiting our lungs; much of the time, particularly when it's working well, we don't even notice it. So although it is perhaps more uncomfortable to do so, it is more revealing to explore moments when our beliefs about ourselves and our actual choices and behaviors are incongruent rather than trying to identify those that are aligned.

While preparing to visit my parents briefly one December in my twenties, I learned that the father of a high school friend had died suddenly. She and I hadn't seen each other in several years, but I quickly let my friend know that I was to be in town and would come to visit to offer comfort and condolences to her and her mother. When I got to my hometown, hopped up on decongestants in an effort to unsuccessfully treat nagging flu symptoms, I discovered that I'd lost the small notecard with my friend's otherwise unlisted address and phone number somewhere between New York and New Jersey. (Weeks later, I would find it behind my desk back at home.) So I did what any reasonable person would do: I went to sleep. I slept much of that weekend, mentally flashing each time I awoke to my grieving friend and the easy justification that I would figure out how to get in touch with her as soon as I felt well. Of course, I did not ever feel well – who feels good about death, even under the best of circumstances? In retrospect, my repeated rationalization was merely an excuse to avoid experiencing an array of difficult emotions. (Perhaps misplacing the notecard was even a subconscious action in service of that avoidance.) I knew in the moment that my choice was probably wrong, but I made it anyway; it was easier to make excuses than to make the hard choice to be present with a grieving family.

But was I really wrong? After all, I was genuinely ill and didn't want to get anyone else sick; our relationship was complicated and historical rather than current or intimate; and surely she was surrounded by plenty of other people whose attention was far more important than mine.

I didn't need someone to tell me. I knew I was wrong. I knew that my inaction was likely to hurt someone I ostensibly cared for, even though my actions indicated otherwise. I also knew that I was wrong for violating my commitment to visit my friend and her mother. And I knew that my feelings about our history, our relationship, our closeness or lack thereof had absolutely no bearing on whether I should follow through with my promise.

Why was disappointing someone I cared for wrong? Well, that disappointment – compounding tremendous grief – probably hurt her. I was behaving badly, but I'm not a monster: I don't want to cause someone hurt.

But why don't I want to cause someone hurt? It seems obvious, but I think it's because I value other people and care about their feelings.

Why? I know what it feels like to experience pain, I don't want to experience unnecessary pain, and I don't want to cause other people to experience unnecessary pain – certainly not with awareness that I am doing so.

But I did. I knowingly and with considerable awareness (can't blame the Benadryl) took an action that I knew was likely to cause someone else hurt. So what did my behaviors suggest *really* mattered to me?

The avoidance of pain.

On reflection, my deep-seated moral belief is that the infliction of pain – especially the intentional infliction of pain – should be avoided at all costs.

Remember, if values tell me what I stand for, then morals tell me what I will not stand for. And I'm pretty sure that I will not stand for the infliction of unnecessary pain.

But then, why had I behaved out of sync with that moral belief?

I hadn't. Perhaps because of immaturity, selfishness, some aspect of my psychology, or (I hope) a momentary and myopic lack of true compassion, I'd calculated that *my* pain was greater than my friend's – and that avoiding my own theoretically greater discomfort outweighed the hurt that I was likely to cause her.

I'd made a choice that was exactly in line with my moral belief.

But because I wasn't mindfully aware of that moral belief, I rationalized that my pain or discomfort was greater, and I made the choice to avoid the greater pain – my own.

In hindsight, it's glaringly obvious to me that my friend's pain was far greater than mine. But as I didn't make the space or yet have the skill or maturity to think through my moral core with clarity and intention, I made a choice that aligned in principle but completely misaligned in practice. And it cost me the relationship, forever.

But how does clarity about my selfishness in a personal relationship more than two decades ago affect my leadership today?

Think back to my team's challenge about whether to take on the client whose business activities seemed to be in contrast with our articulated values. If I know that I hold as core to my morality the notion that I must minimize the infliction of pain, I understand the dilemma differently. I don't want to hurt the employee(s) who are worried about our integrity and our reputation. I don't want to support business activities that cause suffering to others. I don't want to ignore the feelings and needs of people in the client organization who are genuinely asking for help and who have the power to effect change. I don't want to create a false dichotomy between organizations and industries with comparable ethics but better reputations, marketing, and public relations and those without – thereby creating more hurdles and extra work for my employees. And if every option might involve the infliction of some pain, I know that I want to do whatever I can to inflict as little pain as possible. Because to me, that's a moral issue.

Whew. Okay. I haven't answered my difficult question just yet, but I understand morality as an input to my thinking much more clearly – and am more likely to make the tough call intentionally and with empathy as a result.

> ## Difficult Decision: The Philip Guston Retrospective at the National Gallery of Art
>
> "I've always done really well in school and with grades," Kaywin Feldman says, "but I do horribly on standardized tests. I did horribly on my SATs, my GREs. I can always argue the bit in between the true/false and multiple choice questions."
>
> As the first woman in history to lead the National Gallery of Art, she thinks endlessly about questions of cultural relevance, authority, the role of museums, diversity, and representation. But these questions rarely have easy answers.
>
> "Humans are complicated," she explains. "We just seem to want to put everything into a binary – you're either for or against! Something is clear or its opaque! But we're not getting the messy part in the middle. And it's not true or false. There's always somewhere in the middle."[6]
>
> Navigating that complexity and using it to drive the National Gallery into the future has informed her leadership every step of the way so far. "I was hired with

---

[6] Kaywin Feldman, interview with Eric Pliner, February 2021

a clear mandate from the board to put the *national* back in the National Gallery of Art," she says.[7] Since her appointment in 2018, Kaywin faced a different degree of visibility and accompanying scrutiny about her decisions than her predecessors had experienced. With a clear, explicit agenda about making the venerable institution accessible to all Americans, Kaywin's early choices have already influenced the public view of the institution and her leadership.

No decision, though, has challenged Kaywin more as a leader than what to do about Philip Guston. "We were looking at a model of the exhibition and we got to Klan pictures. On a number of occasions, Guston painted cartoon-like hooded figures that allude to the Ku Klux Klan. Most of these come from a certain period in the artist's career. How are we going to treat this material? There was an exhibition of this artist fifteen years ago, and no one said anything about [these images]. That was a period when many art museums were run by white people for a white audience – maybe not explicitly, but it was certainly implicit. I paused on these pictures. Things had changed. We needed to be careful and sensitive about how we presented them. But I was naïve to think that careful and sensitive was enough."

The first period of Kaywin's historic tenure had hardly been easy. She was appointed to lead the institution during an administration as unsupportive of

(Continued)

[7] Zachary Small, "National Gallery of Art Reopens with a New Vision: 'For All the People,' *The New York Times*, May 13, 2021, https://www.nytimes.com/2021/05/13/arts/design/national-gallery-washington-reopen-rebrand.html?.

federal arts institutions as any in modern times.[8] Barely
two years into her role, the COVID-19 pandemic
required the shutdown of the Gallery's physical spaces.
And between those two milestones, allegations of racial
and gender bias in the museum's mission and harassment
in its day-to-day operations were brought to the
attention of the new director and the public.[9]

It was in that context that Kaywin looked at a
planned retrospective of American artist Philip Guston
and realized that she had a difficult decision to make.

More than forty years after Guston's death, his work
is still appreciated for its exploration of topics like "the
seeds of racism and the capacity for evil in all humans."[10]
The artist's daughter, Musa Mayer, noted that her father's
work "dared to hold up a mirror to white America,
exposing the banality of evil and the systemic racism we
are still struggling to confront today."[11] These themes
aligned neatly with Kaywin's commitment to diversity
within the museum's programming and leadership.

---

[8] Eileen Kinsella, "President Trump Is Trying to Eliminate the National Endowment for the Arts – Again – in his Just-Released 2021 Budget Proposal," *Artnet News*. February 10, 2020, https://news.artnet.com/art-world/trump-proposes-eliminating-nea-and-neh-again-1774236.

[9] Peggy McGlone, "National Gallery of Art Director Responds to Allegations of Harassment and Diversity Issues at the Museum," *The Washington Post*, July 17, 2020, https://www.washingtonpost.com/entertainment/museums/national-gallery-of-art-director-responds-to-allegations-of-harassment-and-diversity-issues-at-the-museum/2020/07/17/e6fc5c82-c85b-11ea-8ffe-372be8d82298_story.html.

[10] Kaywin Feldman, "It's Time Museum Leaders Stopped Talking to Themselves – and Started Listening Instead," *Apollo Magazine*, March 24, 2021, https://www.apollo-magazine.com/museum-leadership-empathy-kaywin-feldman/.

[11] Edward Helmore, "Sense or Censorship? Row of Klan Images in Tate's Postponed Show," *The Guardian*, September 27, 2020, https://www.theguardian.com/artanddesign/2020/sep/26/sense-or-censorship-row-over-klan-images-in-tates-postponed-show.

The problem, though, wasn't with the themes; it was with their execution. Twenty-five of the works in the planned exhibition, which had been in development for five years, included cartoonish images of Klansmen. As *The Guardian* notes, "Guston himself said of his Klan images: 'They are self-portraits . . . I perceive myself as being behind the hood . . . The idea of evil fascinated me.'" Kaywin explains, "[Guston] was not a member of the KKK. He was using the image of the KKK to poke at people and get them to question their own feelings about racism and violence."[12]

But, she reflects, "The decision about what to do about [the Guston retrospective] really hit home after the murder of George Floyd and then conversations with our staff. They were so thoughtful about how the images of these clownish figures that allude to the KKK would make people of color feel."[13]

Guston's intent was noble, indeed, but the impact of his particular approach to bringing that intent to life varied dramatically based on the identities and experiences of the viewer – especially in 2020. "People who can intellectualize the paintings, the effect of them, can say, 'Well, his intentions were good, so we should use that perspective,'" Kaywin explains. "But what I have learned yet again through this whole journey is that art is all about people, it's all about emotions, it's messy . . . An individual's feelings [in response] are legitimate even if

(Continued)

---

[12] Ibid.
[13] Kaywin Feldman, interview with Eric Pliner, February 2021.

the first person has good intentions. Good intentions don't negate someone else's feelings."[14]

In her role as the leader of a major institution that planned to exhibit the work, Kaywin sought to listen to her key stakeholders, including her staff, about their perspectives and their feelings. "We had a planning meeting with a very large group of people," she says. "Hearing very loudly from a number of African American employees that they were really unhappy about the show and unhappy that we were proceeding with it affected my thinking . . . He's unquestionably a great artist, and he's had countless exhibitions . . . One African American team member said, 'It's like slicing my arm open again and pouring salt inside. As a Black person, what am I going to learn from this? How am I going to grow? I'm not willing to make that cut unless I'm going to learn from this or grow and there's something there for me.' But we hadn't figured that part out."[15]

Her other stakeholders' views, however, were not monolithic. Employees and visitors were two groups of stakeholders, but what of the Gallery's trustees? Of artists? Of academics in the field? For the *Washington Post*, Pulitzer-Prize – winning art critic Sebastian Smee writes, "Art museums exist, perhaps above all else, to inspire the artists of today and tomorrow."[16] He writes with fervor of "the principle" and "institutional hypocrisy" being of concern to major artists of all

---

[14] Ibid.

[15] Ibid.

[16] Sebastian Smee, "The Philip Guston Controversy Is Turning Artists against the National Gallery," *The Washington Post*. October 16, 2020, https://www.washingtonpost.com/entertainment/museums/philip-guston-exhibition-postponement/2020/10/16/930d74a4-0ef5-11eb-8a35-237ef1eb2ef7_story.html.

identities around the world, and of the risk that postponing the Guston retrospective would pose to the future of the National Gallery's relationships with artists.

So to which stakeholders was Kaywin beholden most? What happens when there is conflict among a leader's role responsibilities? Absent that clarity, Kaywin looked to her personal morals and, perhaps even more critically, to the ethics dictated by the larger context. "Morally, I would have a really hard time asking staff to stand in front of these works without having made sure we discussed them and there was a vehicle to listen and feel and understand each other's views. And I also believed that it wouldn't have been possible," she says. "The majority of our guards – about 85 percent – are African American. I became increasingly aware of what it would mean to ask them to stand eight hours a day and guard these images."[17]

The larger sociopolitical context told a similar story. Ford Foundation president Darren Walker, also a trustee of the National Gallery, explained, "An exhibition organized several years ago, no matter how intelligent, must be reconsidered in light of what has changed to contextualize in real time . . . by not taking a step back, to address these issues, the four museums would have appeared tone-deaf to what is happening in the public discourse about art."[18]

(Continued)

[17] Kaywin Feldman, interview with Eric Pliner, February 2021.
[18] Peggy McGlone, "National Gallery of Art Director Responds to Allegations of Harassment and Diversity Issues at the Museum," *The Washington Post*, July 17, 2020, https://www.washingtonpost.com/entertainment/museums/national-gallery-of-art-director-responds-to-allegations-of-harassment-and-diversity-issues-at-the-museum/2020/07/17/e6fc5c82-c85b-11ea-8ffe-372be8d82298_story.html.

Kaywin agrees. "This is a new kind of alignment for the National Gallery. We hadn't used values to make decisions in this way before. Our key performance indicators came out of the art world and our peers, not out of the audience that we serve. And so if I am judging myself according to how the art world feels, the art world didn't feel too good about that decision. It was a very different kind of decision for the Gallery."[19]

Along with the directors of three other institutions that had planned to show the Guston retrospective, Kaywin made the difficult decision to postpone the exhibition for several years. In doing so, she bought time to reconsider and reposition it in a different sociopolitical and ethical context and to address the implications of the controversy for the National Gallery on a larger scale.

"Context matters," she continues. "If the works had been shown at a different time or in a different kind of institution, maybe they could have been received differently. But the fact that the National Gallery sits next to the Capitol, it sits in the center of power in Washington, [and] it has always been white-led . . . the message that it sends for the National Gallery to say that we can put an image up that references racial terror and it's our right to do it without listening to the people who experience discrimination and the threat of violence – well, that's a very powerful message, but it's one whose time has passed. America has moved along in this discussion."[20]

---

[19] Kaywin Feldman, interview with Eric Pliner, February 2021.
[20] Ibid.

And under Kaywin's leadership, so has the National Gallery. "I've had this technique throughout my career," she explains. "When I have a complicated situation with lots of stakeholders or a conflict with my own emotions, I ask myself what is best for the institution. Nine times out of ten, I find a really clear answer. It may not be best for this person or that person or even for my own feelings. But it's what's best for the institution."[21]

She continues: "If we had gone forward as planned, not only would our staff be put in a really difficult place, but the people standing on Black Lives Matter Plaza in front of the White House are going to be unheard. We say that the National Gallery is 'of the nation and for all the people,' and if that is truly who we are as an institution, then to hurt our staff, to dismiss the thoughts, feelings, and ideas of so many people, well, that's not living up to our vision. So the decision was clear."[22]

A Moral Exercise

One of the best ways to begin to unravel the ways that you perceive right and wrong is to reflect on moments where you witnessed, experienced, or participated in something that you intuitively understand as being wrong. It's not necessarily easy to do this – doing so forces us to look at our own failings – but it can be illuminating to understand moments where there are gaps between what we think we believe and what we actually do.

[21] Ibid.
[22] Ibid.

Think of a time when you did something wrong. It doesn't have to be a big thing – I've done this activity successfully while reflecting on my one and only second-grade transgression, when Mrs. Fulginiti sent five of us to sit in the hall for repeatedly blowing into crayon boxes like musical instruments. But think about something that, on reflection, you consider to be a bad choice.

The following exercise, known as *the five whys*, works best at helping you to identify aspects of your core, underlying morality if you are rigorously honest in reflecting on your experiences and feelings. Being candid with yourself matters more than anything in getting to your moral core. Don't worry about being embarrassed or vulnerable: No one but you is going to check your work here. I certainly won't, and Mrs. Fulginiti, may she rest in peace, died in 2009. So, you're on your own.

Let's try it. Remember: rigorous honesty.

- What, exactly, did you do? Write it down in as much detail as you can remember, no matter how difficult it is to do so. Set the description aside.

- Next, ignore the initial prompt, and instead write down all the reasons why what you did was perhaps *not* wrong. How can you rationalize your choice? Why might it have been totally and completely justified? Why was your choice okay? Set this explanation aside.

- Now, consider: Who or what told you that what you did was wrong? When you tell yourself that what you did was wrong, whose voice do you hear? Is it yours? Someone else's? Both?

- What do those voices or influences mean by "wrong"? Incorrect? Inaccurate? Hurtful? Undermining? Diminishing? Immoral?

- Now, write out a complete clause, starting with "because," that answers this question: Why do you think what you did was wrong?

- Re-read your sentence.

- In response to your sentence, once again, ask yourself, "Why is that wrong?"

- Write out another complete clause in response to that question, once again starting with "because . . ."

- Do that four more times, for a total of five "why" questions and answers.

- What are you left with?

- Ask yourself: What assumptions did I make about what I value? What assumptions did I make about my morality? What assumptions were correct? What surprised me?

- Consider: What do those surprises tell you about your morality – your underlying, inner beliefs about right and wrong? When/how do you generally live and/or behave most in line with your moral view? When is there a gap between your explicit values and your inner moral line?

- What does that gap tell you?

- What questions are you left with?

- Faced with that same situation again, would you make any choices differently? Why or why not? Remember to be real with your answer here.

- Look back at your initial assumptions about your values and morality. What was underneath the surface of your assumptions? Where were you right, and where were your assumptions or conclusions inexact?

- What have you learned about yourself and what you won't stand for? Where are your behaviors incongruous with your beliefs?

- What would enable you to draw greater integrity between what you think, what you stand for, what you won't stand for, and how you behave?

Exercise: Morality and Your Leadership Narrative

How you want to be seen, experienced, and remembered holds useful data about your morality, both underlying and aspirational. It is a natural and human desire to wish to be seen and experienced as perhaps better than we really are. Exploring that impulse can help us to understand who and how we want to be, which can help to inform complex decision-making.

To clarify key aspects of your worldview, ask yourself the following questions without judgment. Some of them will apply directly, others may not. Regardless, observe your reactions to each of the questions:

- When others look back over my leadership, how do I want to be described as a leader? What do I want to stand for?

- What do I personally believe to be the purpose of business? Is it to maximize shareholder value and, by extension, to improve communities and the world by growing collective wealth? Is it to improve communities and the world regardless of growing wealth? Some combination of the two? Something entirely different?

- What do I think leadership really is? What do I see as the purpose of organizations?

- What do I think is the purpose of our business or organization? Is it the same as my view of business or organizations writ large, or is there some nuance based on our size, our geographies, our services?

- What am I willing to sacrifice in service of a desired end state? What am I never willing to sacrifice?

- Remember the lessons from the "Win as Much as You Can" exercise. What do I believe about winning? Does someone have to lose for someone else to win?

To further elucidate your desired moral leadership narrative or brand, try one or more of these exercises:

- Without explicitly mentioning any of your professional achievements, write the **speech that you would like a close friend to give at your memorial service.** Who would make that speech? Why did you choose that person? What would you want that person to say about you? For which qualities do you most wish to be remembered? The reason for leaving out professional achievements is that getting to the source of our personal morality is enhanced by understanding how we operate in the world rather than what we've accomplished. If that's too macabre or the discomfort associated with envisioning your mortality prevents you from focusing on your morality, instead **write the introduction to your receipt of a lifetime achievement award** from the Society for People Doing Good Things. Consider: What does it mean to "Do Good Things"? What does the imaginary "Society" do? Who are these "People"? Why are they awarding you? And what do your definitions tell you about what you believe about good and bad, right and wrong?

- Imagine a **marketing focus group** built entirely around you and your brand as a human being and as a leader. Who should be in the group? Why did you choose those people? What would you want them to say about you? If the participants were asked to create a visual representation of your brand without words, what would you want them to draw? It's okay if what your imaginary focus group participants say isn't necessarily an accurate representation of you one hundred percent of the time; the idea is to paint an aspirational mental picture of you as a moral leader and human being, rather than a precise one. What does your fantasy of this focus group tell you about the brand and leadership story that you hope to have? What does it tell you about how you wish to be seen and experienced and who you want to be?

- Create a simple **720-degree feedback survey** with a few easy questions. A 360-degree feedback survey gathers input from people around you in all directions at work; a 720-degree feedback survey gathers input from people around you at work and in your personal life; it goes all the way around twice. As you're not looking for broad development themes here, keep the questions simple and few. Consider asking things like: How would you describe me as a leader? What do you think matters the most to me? What three essential morals or values would you ascribe to me? When have you seen me make a difficult decision? What did I do well? Make sure you fill out the survey, too, and then examine (or work with a partner to examine) the differences between how you see yourself as a moral leader and how others see you.

- Draw a **map of your leadership journey,** highlighting crucible moments that helped to define you as a leader, what you stand for, and what you do not stand for. Consider moments big and small – they don't all have to be major life changes or dramatic moments, but they should be significant and memorable in helping to shape your mindset or behaviors as a leader. Where does your journey as a leader start? Why did you choose that moment? Why did you select the moments that you've highlighted? What moments did you leave out? Why? What do your choices tell you about what is most important in your journey to developing your leadership?

Once you've entertained these questions or completed one or more of these exercises, ask yourself: How do my answers to these questions reflect my core moral code? What do they say about who I am and who I aspire to be? And how do those perspectives influence my decision-making as a leader?

Key Points

- Values tell us what we stand for; morals tell us what we absolutely won't stand for.
- Many people are uncomfortable with the idea of morality as a component of leadership.
- There is not a single morality; right and wrong are not absolutes.
- Understanding our own morality and using it to drive great decision-making is a humble and

(Continued)

vulnerable act that requires acceptance of our fallibility.

- People generally believe that they are operating morally; when we disagree with that assertion, it is usually because of a difference in our morals, rather than immorality or amorality on the part of either party.

- Leaders can and should help others to think about how our moral codes are applied in our interactions and work.

- Communicating morality, especially in the workplace, is not without risk, but avoiding introspection and communication of morality increases exclusion, demotivation, and disparate treatment.

- Leaders can and should develop skill in understanding morality and its sources and communicating what is directly relevant to their leadership context and role.

- Understanding and staying aware of our morals and where they come from is essential to making decisions with integrity.

- We generally behave in ways that reflect what we really believe. When actions and beliefs don't align, we've probably replaced who we truly are with who we aspire to be.

- We can unravel our core beliefs about right and wrong in part by reflecting on moments where we saw or were a part of something that we intuitively understand as wrong.

- How we want to be seen, experienced, and remembered holds useful data about our morality, both actual/underlying and aspirational.

4

Ethics

If, indeed, morals are internally referenced and externally influenced, ethics represent the converse. They are externally referenced and filtered through the lenses of our individual experiences. Ethics are a staple of functional societies in that they enable coexistence under a set of principles about what's generally okay and what just plumb isn't. Sometimes those ethical principles are codified into laws, which tell us what is allowed and what is not, with the consequence of violation of laws being threat of some sort of punishment. But the relationship between ethics and law is tenuous at best; sometimes laws serve to organize and formalize entirely unethical principles that concentrate power rather than ensuring the greater good.

Keep in mind that ethics aren't norms – they're not merely about "how things are done 'round these parts." They are about the sense of "good" or "bad" attached to those ways of doing things, with the implicit judgment that those characterizations carry. And that general sense of good and bad may look different in different places, across generations, or out in public versus behind closed doors.

Think about cigarette smoking. From one state to the next, from one town to the next – heck, from one restaurant to the next – the rules and norms regarding smoking indoors might vary widely. In one club, bar, or diner, as long as patrons are of age and can choose whether to be present, there may be a clear if unwritten understanding that entering the room means that patrons will be exposed to cigarette smoke. In another, cigarette smoking might not be allowed at all, even if it might've been, in that exact same facility, as recently as a few years ago.

Even in a community where smoking is unpopular and no longer the norm, few would describe the act of smoking a cigarette in and of itself as unethical. (After all, we know enough about the addictive nature of nicotine to understand that smoking cigarettes is not always entirely up to the individual's conscious mind.)[1] Sure, any adult could reasonably describe knowingly smoking cigarettes in a facility that actively and openly bans that activity as unethical – because of its impact on others and the violation of their expectations. In general, though, the ethics and the norms are different here. The norm may be that we don't smoke here, but that doesn't mean we think it's unethical to smoke here.

With that distinction noted, plenty of people today would describe *marketing or selling* cigarettes as unethical, particularly where doing so is in service of generating repeat revenue by engaging younger people in addictive

---

[1] NIDA, *Tobacco, Nicotine, and E-Cigarettes Research Report. Is Nicotine Addictive?*, Research Report, National Institute on Drug Abuse website, 2021, https://www.drugabuse.gov/publications/research-reports/tobacco-nicotine-e-cigarettes/nicotine-addictive.

behaviors at impressionable life stages. That was not likely to be the case even fifty years ago, where marketing and selling cigarettes was broadly understood to be a reasonable component of a legitimate business that sought to engage consumers in a pleasurable activity that was suspected but not widely understood to cause some harm.

Characteristics of Ethics

Ethics are about what is collectively acceptable and considered helpful or harmful. Or even more simply, if morals are about right and wrong and laws are about what's allowed and what's not allowed, ethics are shared views of what's good and what's bad.

A few things about ethics:

- Ethics are contextually dependent and are, therefore, not uniform.
- Ethics change over time.
- Ethics are about shared social acceptability, but they are not about popularity.

So if ethics change and are inconsistent, and the largest group of voices around them might lead us astray, how on Earth are we supposed to figure out the ethical expectations of the context we're operating within?

Let's take these points one by one.

Ethics Are Contextually Dependent and Are, Therefore, Not Uniform

Sometimes spotting differences in ethical frameworks is made easier by crossing geographies. Sometimes those differences are more evident in settings organized by identities that connect to ethical frameworks – faith-based settings, for instance, or educational institutions, industry organizations, or political environments. And sometimes, crossing those invisible boundaries makes less obvious connections between ethical frameworks far more readily apparent. On my first trip to Mumbai, colleagues both living in and originally from India cautioned me against giving money to people living in poverty who were begging in an open market. "You will cause more problems and a lot of chaos if you start handing out money than if you stay stone-faced and keep moving," they explained. "It might seem heartless, but a lot of white Westerners make this mistake and don't realize what they're doing." Heartless, perhaps, considering the currency exchange rate between the US dollar and the Indian rupee, and certainly noticeable to me as an outsider. But the choice is hardly any different from that of countless well-heeled New Yorkers who step past or over people without housing who are clutching signs and coffee cups in midtown Manhattan. In both scenarios, despite different superficial appearances, the prevailing ethos is that it is important to help others in need – unless doing so might cause larger upset or discomfort. Laid out clearly, that prevailing ethos may not reflect on us especially well – but it is the dominant ethical framework nonetheless. Two different settings, similar ethics – both shaped by their specific context and informed by the interrelationship among people existing together in societies. Is it immoral to ignore someone in need? Perhaps. Is it unethical to do so? Certainly not, especially if taking the moral action in the moment could create greater harm.

Take a wildly different example. Is it ethical to develop driverless cars, knowing that some people will absolutely die in them every year? Is it ethical to have cars *with* drivers, knowing that more than 1.3 million people[2] die in them every year? Is it ethical to drive fossil-fuel-powered vehicles when electric vehicles, with lower environmental impact, are available and on the market?

For now, most of us live in a context – and embedded infrastructure – built around the notion that the mobility (physical and economic), accessibility, freedom, independence, pace, and control conferred by individual ownership of fossil-fuel-powered, human-directed motor vehicles generally outweighs the known risk and known harm also conferred by these same vehicles. We depend on them to enable our lives as we know them, and we accept their acknowledged harm in exchange for their acknowledged benefits. That has not always been the case, and perhaps it may not always be the case. Our current context, though, indicates clearly that we generally accept these objects and our dependence on them as ethical – or, at least, as not unethical.

Again, that is not to suggest that driving fossil-fuel-powered, human-directed motor vehicles is *moral*. Plenty of people would argue with clarity and specificity why doing so is immoral. If ethics are externally referenced and internally interpreted – and tell us something about how we live in relation to others – then the general ethic is that our relationship to automobiles may not be ideal, but the good far outweighs the bad.

We always have to start by considering our context. And our ethical context does not always align cleanly with our morality.

The *New York Post* headlines its infamous "Page Six" gossip section with a single line: "If you don't want it on

---

[2]CDC, "Road Traffic Injuries and Deaths – A Global Problem," CDC website, December 14, 2020, https://www.cdc.gov/injury/features/global-road-safety/index.html.

Page Six, don't do it." That is, if you aren't prepared for the public to evaluate whether your actions – or you – are good or bad, right or wrong, then perhaps you shouldn't take those actions. (Whether or not it is moral for the *Post* to publish unconfirmed gossip is another matter, but the general social acceptance of "Page Six" and the like might indicate that it is not inherently unethical – with our third principle about popularity noted as an important caveat.)

To understand your ethical context, think about the quandary from various perspectives, and consider what your reaction to each point of view tells you about the broader context. For example:

- Who is harmed or potentially harmed by the choice that I am making? Who would be harmed by a different choice? Which harm is greater? What would a group of reasonable people say about this choice and its alternatives?

- If a sensationalistic story were to be written about me – or anyone – making this particular choice, what would the headline say? Am I okay with that? How would people I love evaluate that choice – and that headline?

- Who might see my choice as unethical? Why would they say so? What aspects of their identities, experiences, or backgrounds might inform their view? Is it okay to disregard these perspectives? Why or why not? What does my interpretation of contrary views tell me about what matters in my current setting? What does it tell me about what matters less?

- How might someone in a different geography, setting, or culture view this question? How might they evaluate my choices? What would be different? And why?

Remember, you can always go back to asking "why" five times – just as we did in exploring individual morality – to develop greater depth to your understanding.

Ethics Can Change over Time

In Ken Daurio and Cinco Paul's television fantasy *Schmigadoon*, contemporary, bickering couple Melissa and Josh (Cecily Strong and Keegan Michael Key) find themselves trapped in a pastiche of 1940s and 1950s movie musicals while they attempt to work through relationship challenges. Initially resistant to navigating their Technicolor prison, they ultimately seek opportunities to engage with the local characters, including via a picnic basket / bachelorette auction straight out of the musical *Oklahoma*. When Josh stuns the town by bidding a whopping twenty dollars – ten times his nearest competitor – on waitress Betsy (Dove Cameron), an increasingly infuriated and inebriated Melissa protests to the town Mayor (Alan Cumming):

Mayor Menlove: I don't think you quite understand how the picnic basket auction works.

Melissa: Oh, no, I understand how it works, okay? 'Cause these horny sickos are bidding on women like pieces of meat! Okay, well, guess what? Alright! This piece of meat has a brain! And it is filled with thoughts and ideas! So let's get this party started. Who wants to buy this meat basket?

Josh: Mel, please. Get down from there.

Melissa: You get down from there. Shut up. You're just jealous! Oh, and by the way, where we come from, twenty dollars is, like, nothing! It's like a medium pizza, okay? So don't be all impressed!

The ethics of auctioning off the women of the town to raise money for the library seem dubious (or at least comedic) through Melissa's modern-day lens; the ethics of laying down a twenty in an era when most other townspeople stretch to come up with two dollars are equally in question.

It doesn't take a fictional setting, though, to illuminate the ways in which collective ethics change over time. Within many a modern-day American adult lifetime, the general social acceptability of everything from interracial marriage (described, in recent history, as miscegenation or "race-mixing") to same-sex parenting to the capture and tracking of individuals' personal information to recreational marijuana sale and use to the display of sexuality and violence in film to the provision of paid parental leave to romantic relationships in the workplace – and much more – has shifted.

The ethical questions that are most likely to challenge us often contradict aspects of our long-embedded views about how things do or should work. *Long-embedded* implies that we may be using a filter that is from another time or references that no longer reflect contemporary realities.

Ask:

- How might my great-grandparents (or someone of their generation) have felt about this question? My grandparents? My parents? My siblings? Why would they hold different views? What do those differences tell me about them as people? What do those differences tell me about the ethics of the time?

- What developments, tools, technologies, currencies, resources, and understandings – or channels to access those items – exist today that change the ethical context from prior to their existence? For instance, how is our shared understanding of the importance of privacy different now that 97 percent of American adults carry cellphones, most of which are capable of tracking their physical location at any time?. Or, how does the commercial availability of assault weapons affect our ethical interpretation of the right to bear arms as articulated in the US Constitution in 1788? How does the commercial availability of laundry detergent strips affect our understanding of the environmental ethics of buying liquid detergent in large plastic bottles? Does it affect our understanding at all? (Did you even know that laundry detergent strips were a thing?) In all cases, these developments may not change our understanding of the ethical context at all – or they may change our understanding dramatically.

• What could change that would again shift how others in the future might feel about this question?

Exploring what's different about us and our societies between now and then – whenever "then" is – helps to spotlight how ethics can change over time.

Ethics Are about Shared Social Acceptability, but They Are Not about Popularity

This one's a bit murkier. Remember, we know that ethics are about coexistence – how different people interact and what we consider to be good or bad, helpful or harmful, in a given context or society. This notion, plus the fact that they're externally referenced, means that ethics happen outside of the individual – which means that more than one person has to hold a shared view of a principle for it to be indicative of "ethics."

Whether or not those principles reflect "shared social acceptability," however, is contingent on a few questions: First, how big is the group sharing that social acceptability? And second, how broadly held (that is, how widely shared) does the principle need to be?

Any intentionally configured group – and even some that are not configured by design – can have its own ethics. These principles need to be reflective of what is helpful or harmful and shared among people in an effort to drive good – or prevent bad.

But that doesn't mean that they have to be the most popular ideas. Just as it's possible for laws to be unethical, it's fully possible for very popular notions to be wholly unethical. Hackneyed though the reference may be, Nazism was a pretty popular idea that we can readily condemn as unethical.

Ethics aren't necessarily determined by what the majority thinks or allows, although a vocal minority advocating for a shift in ethical framework often finds its ideas becoming more popular over time. (Hence the first point above.) What is sometimes dismissed with a casual catchphrase – think "political correctness," "wokeness," "cancel culture" – is often a marginalized group voicing or advocating for a shift in collective ethics. That might look like moving away from unfettered comedy at the expense of genuine caring (especially when a lack of said caring results in physical or emotional violence); pulling back from giving disproportionate weight to the views of a single dominant identity and sharing social capital more broadly; moving from imprecise or hurtful descriptors to greater self-determination in identity group categorization; or, perhaps most importantly, recognizing that how things are done matters as much as what is done.

The absence of popularity as a criterion for ethics reminds us that in ethical frameworks, not all views are equal. We are not obliged to give the same weighting to all perspectives, particularly those that are harmful. That distinction can appear to run directly counter to efforts for inclusion – creating conditions where all individuals are appreciated for their unique perspectives and experience the psychological safety to share their points of view without fear of retribution. Even when they are popular or simply shared, views that cause harm to others need not necessarily be accounted for in articulating or shaping the ethics of a given system. All the more reason, then, for leaders to find ways to convey the moral expectations and ethical framework of a system as explicitly as possible when engaging individuals who hope to join that system – lest there be a mismatch that results in harm.

Difficult Decision: Hip Hop Public Health and the American Beverage Association

When Lori Rose Benson[3] joined Hip Hop Public Health (HHPH) as its chief executive officer, she brought together eclectic interests, including her lifelong personal passions for music (she plays the violin in Whitney Houston's "I Believe in You and Me" video), health (she was the founding executive director of the Office of Fitness & Health Education with the New York City public schools, the largest school system

---

(Continued)

[3]All quotes from Lori Rose Benson in this chapter are from an interview with Eric Pliner, August 2021.

in America), and fitness (she once taught the macarena to millions of viewers on *Live with Regis and Kathie Lee*). And she was hired to execute on the vision, plan, and foundation created by Columbia University neurologist Dr. Olajide Williams and legendary hip hop artist Doug E. Fresh, who built the organization to use the arts to reach Black and Latino kids with life-changing public health messages.

Benson's personal desire to use evidence-based, scientific strategies to support health improvement, particularly with Black and Latino young people who have so often been ignored by the field, is informed by an ethical drive to take the judgment out of public health. "So often," she explains, "public health messages are judgmental – especially of the people they purport to support – and completely miss the mark in terms of engagement. How can we use methods that truly engage people in health literacy and behavior change in a really positive way, not by using scare tactics? We harness the power of music, learning, storytelling, and gamification – all strategies that advertisers know how to use well – to improve health literacy and enable behavior change in a positive way."

With that clear purpose and service orientation in mind, plenty of individuals and organizations of all kinds were keen to partner with HHPH. Some made for easy connections: The HHPH nonprofit was specifically incorporated to enable collaboration with former First Lady Michelle Obama's Let's Move initiative and the Partnership for a Healthier America. Collaborating artists like Darryl DMC McDaniels,

Jordin Sparks, Chuck D, and Ashanti signed up to record tracks and offer support.

At the time, Benson explains, HHPH had "a ton of in-kind support but very little funding, except for an occasional corporate grant or government-backed research and operations funding." The HHPH board was ready and eager to take its impact and visibility to another level. That's when the American Beverage Association, the trade association that represents producers and distributors of non-alcoholic beverages, offered financial support.

The two organizations had worked together previously alongside the Partnership for a Healthier America on the "Drink Up" campaign, where HHPH created "River of Life," a song about choosing water. And through the Balance Calories Initiative, ABA had led an industrywide commitment to reduce Americans' consumption of calories from beverages by 20 percent by 2025. But even with that statement and with bottled water as the fastest-growing segment of the American beverage industry, the overwhelming majority of beverage industry products remained known contributors to childhood and adulthood caloric consumption: carbonated soft drinks, fruit beverages, and sports drinks. It was clear why ABA would want to sponsor HHPH; but was it ethical for HHPH to accept support from a sponsor whose success was a direct contributor to the behaviors that the organization existed to address? And how did those ethics align or conflict with HHPH leaders' personal views of right and wrong – and the responsibilities of their roles?

(Continued)

The ethics question wasn't new to Benson. In her previous role with the New York City Department of Education, she remembered a time when vending machines were omnipresent in public schools. She recognized the concerted community and health leadership efforts that had gone into taking them out – even while students, teachers, and administrators panicked about losing a key source of fundraising for their communities. Schools desperately needed the revenue conferred by candy sales and soda vending machines, but New York City was facing a childhood obesity crisis that Benson and her team were charged with addressing. To her surprise, industry leaders were listening. They began to make changes and respond to the social commitment that schools were making, while still offering ways for schools to earn cash from their products – aligning the environment to their business agenda and the city's desired health outcomes for its young people. "That experience expanded my own view of public–private partnerships and how to have a wider range of voices at the same table, having the same conversation," Benson explains. "That made me think that there could be a way to push everyone in a direction that was better for all of us."

The fact that many industries, including the beverage industry, had made major changes to their ways of engaging young people made the question less morally murky, too. "What was happening when we were kids, or even twenty or thirty years ago, with targeted advertising to very young children, those practices don't exist anymore. This industry association has made a change to its approach, and that change has undergone objective evaluation in a credible way."

So it wasn't *morally* wrong to accept money from ABA, and HHPH leaders' role in raising financial support for the organization to meet its aspirations was crystal clear. But helping young people to consume less of the product hawked by ABA was also in line with the leaders' role. So was accepting the funds *ethical*?

Like many public health organizations with a harm-reduction philosophy, HHPH isn't absolutist in its approach. "One of the philosophies of Hip Hop Public Health, especially in nutrition literacy, is called 'Go, Slow, Whoa!'" Benson explains. "We never describe any food or beverage as bad all the time; it's like a traffic light. 'Go' foods are fine, 'Slow' need a bit more consideration and moderation, and 'Whoa!' is an occasional treat."

That philosophy seems to extend to its partners. "Even if the products contribute to the overall obesity crisis and have played a part in that," she notes, "we want those people to be at the table. My ethos is that it's better to work with people than against people. So how do we keep moving forward towards a totality of better options?"

Starting in 2017, the American Beverage Association became a sponsor of Hip Hop Public Health – with a caveat from the recipient. "Our board was clear that it was not comfortable with the ABA directly sponsoring programs in schools, and ABA wasn't asking to do that," Benson explains. "They were okay – even excited

(Continued)

about – ABA supporting us to develop and implement a national engagement plan, attend and speak at conferences, and offer workshops with health literacy resources to expand our reach to more children and families." And their efforts didn't end there – in parallel, ABA was working with community groups to retool nutrition labels, making them easier to read and understand, adjusting serving sizes, and more.

The challenge in answering a difficult ethical question involving a partner is that the question isn't really ever fully and permanently resolved. Now, Hip Hop Public Health is preparing a new campaign, this time focused on the many guises of sugar – including its inclusion in most beverages other than water, milk, coffee, or tea. So how do their partners and funders at ABA feel about that? And will Benson even ask?

"I don't think we have to consult with every one of our partners on every single initiative," she explains. "We're explicit about who we are, what we stand for, what we won't stand for, what we do and what our focus is." But that's not all. "The thing is, we *want* to engage them. We want them to know what we're thinking, what we're building, how our health literacy curriculum is bolstered with more resources around products – including products that they create. That's part of being a good partner – we make sure that we proactively have the conversation and stay in the dialogue. Not every conversation is comfortable, but the more explicit we are, the easier it is to align."

How has the choice to accept funds from the American Beverage Association changed Hip Hop

Public Health? It's probably brought the organization's imperative for checking its morals, the ethical context, and its multiple (and sometimes conflicting) roles into stark relief. "We approach everything with curiosity about having a conversation, understanding where people are coming from," Benson says. "We always look at the mission and vision of the funder *and* of the proposed campaign, and consider how that aligns with our mission, vision, strategic goals, and values. Are they on a path to building health literacy and healthier behaviors, or is this just about marketing? Then we have conversations internally, with our team and our board."

Benson and her team have built some scaffolding around the process, too. "We created a revenue guiding policy and principles to help that consideration along," she explains. "We're more open about things that are not youth-facing; there, the guardrails aren't the same. We're all about empowering young people with knowledge and skills to make healthier choices. Our top stakeholders are young people and their families, and so the level of scrutiny is different."

The more they explore these difficult questions, Benson says, the easier it gets. "We accept funds from lots of individuals and companies, but we make sure they are also supporting the behaviors that are essential to who we are and what we do. Where there are exceptions – and there absolutely are – we make sure we are vetting not just a particular campaign, but also the business practices of the sponsoring organization."

(Continued)

She offers an illuminating analogy: "We work with a lot of brilliant artists, some of whom have a particular brand out in the world. Some of them have a past reputation, and it's not always in exact alignment to what schools or parents want to see. But understanding where people are now, where artists are now, where companies are now, the commitment to health equity and social justice, to understanding public health, to understanding racism as a public health issue – today is what matters. There are always opportunities for every one of us to evolve. That is literally the premise of our work, that we can all grow and change for the better."

The Ethics of Leading Politically

There is absolutely no such thing as apolitical leadership. That naive fantasy is from a different era that doesn't exist anymore. The pretense of no opinion is, in and of itself, an opinion – and your employees and customers know it.

This shift represents a marked change in our ethical context. For decades, leaders followed an ethos of political agnosticism, enabling customers and employees to project their own views and associations onto a brand or company and allowing appreciation or rejection of that brand or company to be based on its products or services, nothing more. But with a wealth of information available at their fingertips, individual stakeholders are more likely than ever to align themselves with organizations that represent their perspectives – and to attempt to influence said alignment by threatening defection from those that don't.

The change creates a conundrum for individual leaders seeking to reconcile differences in their personal perspectives and their role responsibilities by looking to the ethical context. Where previous generations of leaders could find relief from the conflict by relying on that philosophy of avoiding politics (except those that clearly and directly affected the operations of their companies), current executives don't have that luxury. With unprecedented speed, today's stakeholders leverage everything from central office locations to affect state politics (as with threatened boycotts of Coca-Cola and Delta in response to voting laws in Georgia), investment funds to influence international policies (as in the divestment of New Jersey pensions from Unilever in reaction to the Ben & Jerry's response to the Israeli-Palestinian conflict), and advertising buys to influence media outlets (as in the Lexus and Samsung withdrawals from sponsorship of Fox News' *Tucker Carlson Tonight*).

Leaders at companies like Coinbase and Basecamp learned the hard way about the impact of attempting political agnosticism. After their respective CEOs issued statements insisting that each company would only focus on issues specifically related to their industries and operational content, Coinbase lost more than 5 percent of its workforce and Basecamp lost upward of 30 percent, ultimately requiring an apology from its CEO to quiet the noise that his proclamation had created. The outcry was not entirely surprising to anyone keeping tabs on our collective societal shifts; especially for any stakeholders who experience identity-related marginalization or have family members who do – which, by the way, is most people – the notion of being apolitical is both political and dismissive of their lived experiences in and out of the workplace. To those employees, customers, and investors, the idea of separating a political stance from their role in and relationship to a business is unimaginable – and potentially impossible. And that desire to align to employers, brands, and companies that reflect individual and communal values, identities, and expectations is more pronounced than ever.

It's not as though the cop-out of addressing only directly related political issues absolves leaders of criticism or the perception of partisanship, anyway. When an owner of Jackson Hole Mountain Resort, Patagonia's "largest customer in [the Wyoming] area," sponsored a fundraiser headlined by three national politicians with poor environmental records – plus social priorities that conflicted with the company's stated stances – the outdoor sportswear company cancelled its contract to sell products at the resort.[4] "Those that know us in Jackson Hole are aware that we make business decisions and build relationships in alignment with our values and advocacy efforts," Patagonia's spokesperson told *The Washington Post*.[5] That didn't stop the criticism from all sides, accusing Patagonia of playing "partisan politics"[6] on the one hand, and of hypocrisy and performativity for withdrawing a business relationship over environmental conservation while still using petroleum products in their manufacturing.[7]

[4]Angus M. Thuermer, "Patagonia Dumps Jackson Hole Ski Resort after Far-Right Fundraiser," *WyoFile*, August 18, 2021, https://www.wyofile.com/patagonia-dumps-jackson-hole-ski-resort-after-far-right-fundraiser/.
[5]Timothy Bella, "Clothier Patagonia Boycotts Ski Resort after Owner Hosted GOP Fundraiser with Marjorie Taylor Greene," *Washington Post*, August 21, 2021, https://www.washingtonpost.com/politics/2021/08/21/patagonia-boycott-wyoming-resort-greene/.
[6]D. Hunter Schwarz, "Patagonia Boycotts Wyoming Ski Resort over Owners' Republican Fundraiser," *Deseret News*, August 20, 2021, https://www.deseret.com/2021/8/20/22633158/patagonia-boycotts-wyoming-ski-resort-over-owners-republican-fundraiser-freedom-caucus-trump.
[7]Leo Sigh, "Hypcritical Patagonia Boycotts Wyoming Ski Resort While Still Using Petroleum-Based Products in Their Clothing," *Leo Sigh*, August 23, 2021, https://leosigh.com/hypocritical-patagonia-boycotts-wyoming-ski-resort-while-still-using-petroleum-based-products-in-their-clothing/.

Leaders can't win, it seems, which potentially makes the Coinbase and Basecamp approach all the more appealing. If we're bound to get it wrong no matter what we do, that approach seems to ask, why not just dispense with the distractions and get back to the work of our work? Why bother taking stances and making statements and backing initiatives and condemning legislation if all it's going to do is make someone angry every time and leave us with boycotts and lost revenue and social media firestorms and employee turnover?

The answer is that our contemporary ethical context demands it. Leaders have to be educated about the issues that matter to our mix of stakeholders. It's among the responsibilities of the role of leader now. (More on that in the next chapter.) We can no longer expect to use passive contentment as an indicator of satisfaction among our constituents. In today's world, ensuring engagement with, belief in, alignment to, even passion for our organizations and our products and services demands knowing and articulating our values – and taking actions that reflect integrity in living them.

Waiving Ethics

I'm not enough of a linguist to know whether "ethics waiver" is technically an oxymoron, but at the very least, the definition seems inherently contradictory. If ethics are a set of principles about what's generally okay and what isn't, about what we collectively consider to be helpful or harmful, then the possibility of waiving the contents of an ethics statement suggests that they aren't actually ethics at all. They may still be principles and they can certainly serve as guidelines, but if it's possible to determine that what's not okay, according to that statement that we've so carefully crafted, is actually okay sometimes, then we might want to get the red pen ready.

The 2017 beginning of Donald Trump's presidential administration represented a marked shift in the US federal government approach to ethics rules and requirements. After issuing "five times any many waivers [of ethics policies] in his first four months as Obama did,"[8] Trump operated with a vague approach to ethics that existed largely behind closed doors, with discussion limited largely to the individuals involved and those officials responsible for granting waivers.

When Joe Biden became the US president, he and his administration sought to differentiate themselves from their predecessors through a series of ethics-related policies and practices both legitimate and performative. In January of 2021, shortly after his inauguration, the Biden administration released an "Executive Order on Ethics Commitments by Executive Branch Personnel."

There's some good content in the Order's pledge for people who care about transparency as a component of ethics:

> I recognize that this pledge is part of a broader ethics in government plan designed to restore and maintain public trust in government, and I commit myself to conduct consistent with that plan. I commit to decision-making on the merits and exclusively in the public interest, without regard to private gain or

---

[8]Matthew Yglesias, "Trump Has Granted More Lobbyist Waivers in 4 Months than Obama Did in 8 Years," *Vox*, June 1, 2017, https://www.vox.com/2017/6/1/15723994/trump-ethics-waivers.

personal benefit . . . I commit to ethical choices of post-Government employment that do not raise the appearance that I have used my Government service for private gain, including by using confidential information acquired and relationships established for the benefit of future clients.[9]

Under the executive order, waivers are granted for two reasons: "The application of the restriction is inconsistent with the purposes of the restriction," and/or "that it is in the public interest to grant the waiver." The latter reason is clearer than the former, which is the stated premise for most exceptions. But even media watchdogs scrutinizing the waivers granted to Biden administration officials are careful to note that such officials were upfront about the waivers and their reasons for seeking them; that these waivers were filed ahead of Senate confirmation hearings; and that none of them came as a surprise.[10]

Neither your political affiliation and alignment nor your view of the ethics of either administration have much bearing on the salient point here. Exceptions to ethics rules tell us as much about the content of those rules (and their genuine legitimacy as ethics) as the rules themselves. Exceptions can be unnerving for those on the receiving end of an organizational ethics framework, as they appear to undermine the full credibility of the framework. But they can also be illuminating, as they can sharpen our understanding of the essential ethics that actually exist beneath our stated intent.

---

[9] Joseph R. Biden Jr., *Executive Order on Ethics Commitments by Executive Personnel*, The White House, January 20, 2021, https://www.whitehouse.gov/briefing-room/presidential-actions/2021/01/20/executive-order-ethics-commitments-by-executive-branch-personnel/.

[10] Lachlan Markay, "Revealed: Biden's Ethics Exceptions," *Axios*, August 29, 2021, https://www.axios.com/biden-team-ethics-waivers-aa1053f7-67fb-478d-aa7c-5e3c37bfee70.html.

An Exercise in Exceptions

To ascertain the exceptions to your ethical context, start by clarifying the boundaries of that context. Are you thinking about the ethics of your office? Your organization? Your industry or field of practice? Your community? Country? Something else?

Next, determine which principle(s) you are consulting as the representation of the ethics of this context. Is there a code of ethics? A values or principles statement that serves as a general indicator of prevailing ethics? Are you left to interpret what's generally okay and what's generally not? Or does the representation consist of some mix of these?

Finally, consider the specific content of the applicable ethical principle. Can you look at it on its own, or does a complete consideration require understanding the intersection of this principle with the others that constitute the total ethical context? (That last point may be a tough one in theory, but it makes more sense when you have a tangible question in mind.)

Once you've established a reasonable understanding of your ethical context – that is, the general and specific principle(s) about what is helpful and what is harmful in your identified setting – you can begin to think about exceptions.

Ask yourself:

- When, in this specific context, would I consider overriding, violating, or outright ignoring this principle? When would I be okay with someone else overriding, violating, or ignoring this principle?

- What kinds of conditions might have to exist for me to make the choice to override, violate, or ignore this principle? How many different examples can I come up with?

- What do my examples have in common? Do they reflect a different and equally explicit ethical principle that might take precedence over this one? Do they represent an implicit ethical principle that should be made explicit? Are they situation-specific, with no consistent theme?

Let's try a real example.

Perhaps the best known and most oft-cited ethical principle is that of nonmaleficence, more commonly articulated as "do no harm." It's a core component of the codes of ethics of lots of fields and professions, including medicine, social work, psychology, education, humanitarian aid, nursing, and cross-disciplinary human subjects research. Nonmaleficence is often – albeit not always – combined with beneficence, which is to say that alongside not doing any harm, most professionals should also try to do some good. Fair enough.

But what are the cases in any of these fields – or in our own leadership – when we might violate the ethic of doing no harm, and might instead acknowledge that doing some harm serves the ethic of doing some good? Is that the only time when violating the principle of nonmaleficence is okay? When is doing no harm overridden by some other principle? What do those examples have in common? And what do those commonalities tell us about the ethic of "do no harm"?

- A dentist pulls a tooth to prevent decay from spreading. Getting the tooth pulled hurts, which constitutes harm, as might not having a tooth (er, especially if it's in the front).

- To cut losses and stay within budget, a business leader pulls the plug on a project that a team has toiled away on for six months, saving cost – and likely some jobs – in the process. Throwing away extensive work from devoted employees likely causes harm, however, particularly where those employees made personal and familial sacrifices to complete that work on time.

- A social worker removes a child from a home where she is not receiving adequate care, getting her access to more consistent instrumental support but denying her daily contact with her parents and some members of her immediate family, undoubtedly causing some emotional harm.

- A nurse protects a family from exposure to a highly contagious, often fatal illness by denying access to the room where a family member is dying. There is inevitable psychological harm in preventing a family from seeing their loved one in his final hours.

Ethics and Judgment

I once attended a dinner where I was seated next to the founder and CEO of an up-and-coming record label that had gotten a lot of attention for several of its breakout artists. Upon hearing that I had experience in working with leaders on preventing workplace harassment, he peppered me with questions related to issues among the staff in his rapidly growing workplace. "This keeps coming up," he said, "so I have this idea that I think will help with the sexual harassment claims. What if I put up signs that tell people what's going to happen? Then they know it's not actually harassment? Like, 'It's not harassment – it's a compliment!' Or 'We love crude jokes and sexual humor!' Or 'You've been warned!'"

I suggested that he might want to hire a human resources department and a lawyer instead.

There is a critical if imperfect relationship between ethics and judgment. Sometimes, a lapse in judgment is a manifestation of a weak ethical framework; sometimes, a lapse in ethics is a manifestation of poor judgment. And sometimes, well, the relationship is symbiotic – with, er, signs everywhere.

What is judgment, anyway, and how do we differentiate "good" judgment from "bad" judgment?

Our firm defines *judgment* this way:

> The characteristics and abilities that enable us to see, learn, understand, and apply our understanding across a variety of practical and theoretical contexts. This includes reading and making coherent decisions within ambiguous environments while anticipating changes, assessing and applying appropriate depth and accuracy, working through both simple and complex problems, and being able to adopt new and nuanced perspectives beyond the here and now.

That's a long way of explaining three constructs that explain how we make judgments: framing, or how we understand, envision, and articulate situations; recognizing, or how we spot and resolve issues; and analytical rigor, or the depth and accuracy with which we build our understanding of situations. Alongside drive and influence, strong judgment is one of three core indicators of long-term leadership potential.

What this model of understanding judgment recognizes is that we may all come to different conclusions based on available data, but that the conclusions that we draw – which are, ultimately, fairly subjective – matter less than how we get to them. That's an essential component of building and cultivating an ethical leadership style, dynamic, or culture, even (especially?) when we are fundamentally unlikely to interpret the same data in the same way. The leader's ability to cultivate an environment where people listen for and empathize with different perspectives, and then pursue ways forward with clarity, specificity, and nuance, reflects good judgment and a strong ethical framework.

An Ethics Exercise

The risk of so-called social desirability – that is, giving the answer that we think will make us look good – is one that clouds lots of social science research. How can we make sure that respondents to hypothetical scenarios are truly representing what they would do when faced with a real-life ethical dilemma? And when we're the respondents, how can we be sure that we're being completely authentic, despite internal and external pressures, real or imagined, to say that we'd do the "right" thing?

We can't, and that gap creates a terrific opening to build our understanding of existing ethical frameworks and their relationship to or distance from our aspirational ethics.

Take any one of the following scenarios or try each one in turn and see what you can learn about your own ethical frameworks and the contexts within which you operate. Remember, ethics are about what is generally accepted across the specific context as being good or bad, helpful or harmful. We're not considering right and wrong – morals – but okay and not okay:

- Is it ethical for a leader who is privately predicting a performance downturn (using publicly available economic indicators) to openly declare optimism to investors about her company's upcoming performance?

- Is it ethical for an individual who knows that he plans to move to another country for family reasons in eight months to accept a leadership role with a location requirement (and hope to perform so successfully that he can influence the company to allow him to relocate later)?

- Is it ethical for a company to release a new application today if they know that said application is likely to be easily adapted by a secondary market to rapidly glean private customer data from internet browsers without the end user's knowledge?

- Is it ethical for a board of directors to run a CEO succession interview process if they know that they have selected a successor ahead of that process?

- Is it ethical for an identified high-potential employee to participate in a selective internal leadership development program knowing that she intends to leave for another company?

- Is it ethical for a company to offshore 40 percent of its workforce to an international market with lower-cost talent?

- Is it ethical for a company that is following all applicable local, state, and federal laws to avoid paying any corporate tax?

- Is it ethical for a company to market at a discount and as "final sale," with neither explanation nor warranty, a product that is known to fail upward of 40 percent of the time?
- Is it ethical to make a small, off-the-books payment to move one's products to the front of the queue in a delayed international supply chain, knowing that one's company will otherwise be unable to fulfill its customer demand and would have to lay off hundreds if not thousands of workers?

Reflection Questions

- Why did you answer as you did? What were the push and pull factors driving you toward one response or the other?
- How did you define the word *ethical*? How, if at all, did your definition shift as you worked through the questions?
- What did you learn about yourself and your view of your current ethical context as you explored the questions?
- What, if anything, surprised you? What do you want to see be different?
- Which answers would you be proud to share with other people? Which ones would you be more cautious about sharing? With whom would you feel most confident sharing your ethical lens? What do the people on (or off) that list tell you about your view of ethics?

Difficult Decision: Bigger or Better? Leading for the Enterprise at Shire Pharmaceuticals

When Ginger Gregory became chief human resources officer of Shire Pharmaceuticals in February 2014, she knew that part of her role would be to support the organization and its people through a period of extraordinary growth. That meant addressing comprehensive systemic needs, from human resources systems and infrastructure to organizational design to leadership and culture and everything in between. Leading those changes was part of the appeal of the role: Gregory had found a sweet spot in industrial and organizational psychology after discovering herself too impatient to work with individuals and too overwhelmed by the scope of social psychology. Organizations were a manageable size, with a big opportunity to have significant impact as a professional and as a leader.[11]

As Shire grew both organically and through acquisitions, the transformation and further professionalization of the human resources function was a top priority. "We had to raise the strategic impact of the HR team," Gregory explains, "by moving from managing transactions to serving as true business leaders." Though the team was well on its way on a journey of creating real ownership of talent processes among Shire's leaders and managers, the existing systems weren't enough.

(Continued)

---

[11]All quotes from Ginger Gregory in this chapter are from an interview with Eric Pliner, September 2021.

"We had to introduce a new human capital management (HCM) system," Gregory says, "and it had to be something very easy to use for all employees and managers. We had to move into the modern century! Employees and managers needed to be able to update their own personnel information; they also needed to manage core HR processes like performance management, year-end compensation planning, reporting lines, opening new roles, and more."

As the business grew more complex and expanded its international operations, the importance of creating consistent global processes that facilitated talent movement and a common approach to management was even more essential. Shire's executive committee supported the introduction of a new human capital management system, as did the remunerations committee of the board of directors. This was a high-profile project with a number of critical stakeholders.

And it was also pretty dull – at first, anyway. "Personally, implementing an HR system is not the most fun thing about any HR job," Gregory laughs. "I was [eager] to focus on the cultural and systemic transformation and for all of us not having to worry about operational things. So making this our entire team's priority for a whole cycle was disappointing – it wasn't much fun for me or my team."

That is, until it worked. "We were humming," Gregory recalls. "Despite being 'just a system,' it was fundamental to our human capital strategy and to our business strategy, not to mention our operating model, our goals, and our budget. Keeping the HR team and others on board and engaged with the system was a leadership challenge and a great opportunity for the HR leadership team. And everyone was happy! Managers didn't have to wait for HR anymore. They could do the work themselves."

"Once people learned what they could do," she continues, "not only were our HR colleagues pleased, but employees were pleased, managers were pleased. Everyone suddenly had access to all of this information and could manage their teams – even from their cell phones." As the acceptance and use of the system increased and spread throughout the organization, end users went from curious to appreciative to dependent on functionality they hadn't even known they'd needed.

The system's flexibility was also part of its appeal, as Shire's plans to continue rapid growth showed no signs of stopping. "Fast-forward a few months," Gregory recalls, "and Shire had decided to acquire Baxalta." This acquisition was no small undertaking: Baxalta had more than three times the number of employees as Shire, and the combined companies were projected to deliver more than $20 billion in annual revenues.[12] And from a systems perspective, the integration was complicated. Baxalta had only spun off from Baxter a mere six months prior to the announcement of Shire's planned acquisition and was still heavily reliant on the previous owner for

(Continued)

[12]Baxalta Incorporated and Shire plc, "Shire to Combine with Baxalta, Creating the Global Leader in Rare Diseases," press release, January 11, 2016, https://www. prnewswire.com/news-releases/shire-to-combine-with-baxalta-creating-the-global-leader-in-rare-diseases-564834551.html.

many of its systems, including human capital management.

That wasn't a huge deal, Gregory thought. "A key principle for the successful integration was to use the best of both companies," she says, and Shire's HCM system had been a roaring success. "If it's better from Shire, do it this way, if it's better from Baxalta, do it that way. That was the guidance for pretty much every process. I felt great about it. Initially it seemed obvious that we would transfer all 23,000 [Baxalta] employees directly over to our system, using our approach."

But the team's new colleagues at Baxalta had very strong and passionate views about how to properly implement the exact same HCM software – and they were down the path of planning their own implementation. "Some aspects of their configuration were a bit better, others were worse," Gregory recalls. Either way, someone was going to be unhappy. "As the acquirer, we had to decide what to do. We had numerous debates and discussions, but in the end, I had to make the decision."

Not that she could be objective. "I was personally extremely proud of and invested in the progress that we'd made as a company and as a function," Gregory says. "We'd really needed to move our function from being transactional and administrative to being full partners to the business. And we had done it. I was so proud of the progress we were making. But suddenly we had 23,000 more people."

With a super-fast integration strategy looming, Gregory ultimately made a tough choice. "I decided that we would go backwards for the historical employees and leaders of Shire," she says. "We'd start over again from scratch on a large, year-long project to implement a system for the entire new company." That meant that all of her happy stakeholders would lose all of the access to data to which they'd grown accustomed – not to mention the information, tools, and resources to manage their teams – while the organization started over in support of the joint enterprise.

"I had to do it," Gregory says. "I had to disappoint 7,000 people to play the long game of having us be one company."

She didn't mince words in the messaging. "I had to tell them, 'We're going to throw out all of your work. And all of the things that you were able to do quickly without calling HR, our huge growth towards eliminating bureaucracy and unnecessary time, well, it's only going to half-work for the next year. We have to put in a brand new version. And in the short run, it's going to go backward.'"

It didn't go over well. "There was a lot of mess and confusion. People said, 'You can't do this. We spent all of this time, all of this money.' Our IT function, our HR function – people said to me, 'I spent years of my life doing this work and we spent literally hundreds of thousands of dollars doing it, and now you're telling me we have to put it on hold and start all over again? When it's working?'"

"The workforce of Shire had been my key stakeholder," Gregory recalls. That was a role that she

(Continued)

didn't take lightly. "Work is really important to me," she explains, "and my team and colleagues were always really important to me – 99% of the people I was interacting with had become close friends. I respected them, I enjoyed them."

"I knew it wouldn't be easy," she says. "It took a significant amount of time and energy to explain this decision to our senior leaders, our board of directors, our managers. It was in the best interests of the organization in the long run, but it was very hard and challenging to tolerate capability going down for a full year in order to bring everyone up to where we'd wanted to be for that long run."

Other stakeholders were less aggrieved. "A lot of what we were doing was happening in the steering committee, but with lots of input from finance and legal and folks in the M&A team. The CEO was pretty hands off about it, but the board represented another set of stakeholders to manage. They were checking up on everything – I'd been updating the [remunerations committee] on everything, and suddenly we were going backwards. Still, they generally understood – their job is to have the long game in mind."

So how did Gregory's decision pan out in the long run?

It didn't. Amidst a push from the CEO several months later to completely restructure the combined organization yet again – at a moment when Gregory felt that Shire's people desperately needed stability – she opted to move on. "What he wanted to do, it was going to rock the boat yet again," she said. "There was dissention among our people and serious engagement and retention issues. I struggled with it, but I had to stand up for what I believed in and stand up for the organization. We'd spent months and months planning to bring people together, and we were finally in a good place in terms of setup and goals and ambitions. It didn't seem right to disrupt all of it again. I couldn't do it." She left Shire Pharmaceuticals in April 2017.

Ultimately, the combined companies' plan for fully integrating its technologies was quickly rendered moot. Just over a year after Gregory's departure, Tokyo-based biopharmaceutical company Takeda announced its intention to acquire Shire, and the deal was complete within nine months. Shire's legacy processes, infrastructure, systems – and many of its people – were no more.

Key Points

- Ethics are externally referenced and filtered through the lenses of our individual experiences.
- Ethics are a staple of functional societies in that they enable coexistence under a set of principles about what's generally okay and what just plumb isn't. They are about collective acceptability and shared views of help and harm, good and bad.
- Ethics and laws are not the same.

(Continued)

- Ethics are contextually dependent and are, therefore, not uniform.

- Ethics change over time.

- Ethics are about shared social acceptability, but they are not about popularity. The majority view is not necessarily the ethical view.

- Ethics do not necessarily align with morality.

- Making ethical decisions is likely to disappoint or anger some people who have a different view of the prevailing ethic.

- Our contemporary ethical context demands that leaders understand the relationship between leadership and politics.

- Leaders must be prepared to take a public, political stance, even on issues seemingly unrelated to their work. The absence of an articulated political perspective is nonetheless experienced by key stakeholders as a political perspective.

- What we are willing to exempt or allow tells us more about our underlying ethics than what we say we stand for.

5

Role Responsibilities

What is the difference between a job and a role?

We use this language interchangeably, but these are not simple synonyms. While a job consists of one or more tasks for which its holder accepts responsibility, a role goes beyond that definition to encompass the broader context or ecosystem. Execution of a job can exist on its own, with deliverables that define its successful or unsuccessful execution. A role, however, exists in relationship to other people, not just to outcomes. A job has requirements; a role has requirements and interpersonal dynamics.

Perhaps obviously, clarifying the requirements and expectations of one's role is essential to effective leadership. Is the leader obligated to fulfill all requirements and manage all interpersonal dynamics equally? What results do different players expect? When and how do their expectations outweigh those of others in a stakeholder constellation? In other words, should employees, customers, and communities be treated with the same regard as owners and investors? And what happens when their respective needs are in conflict?

The word *role* comes originally from theater, from the literal roll of paper upon which an actor's lines were written. Like an actor in a play, someone who holds a role in an organization has an audience looking to her to convey a message, tell a story, enable a change, or inspire an emotional reaction. Every person in a role has others depending on her, including customers and colleagues in more or less senior positions. Her colleagues' ability to perform their own roles is contingent not only on her ability to interface with them skillfully but also on how well she can communicate with others, who may or may not be in the same physical spaces.

The people who depend on one another in an organization are called stakeholders, and they tell us a lot about with and for whom we are working. In *servant leadership*, employees are the critical stakeholders, letting their leaders know what they need to be able to do their jobs as successfully as possible. *Stakeholder capitalism* suggests that the mission of business leaders is "serving not only shareholders, but also customers, suppliers, workers, and communities."[1]

The repositioning of stakeholders (those who have a stake in the actions taken by an organization) as front and center above shareholders (those who own shares of the profits of an organization) is a pretty recent concept. For

---

[1] Vivan Hunt, Bruce Simpson, and Yuito Yamada, "The Case for Stakeholder Capitalism," McKinsey, November 12, 2020, https://www.mckinsey.com/business-functions/strategy-and-corporate-finance/our-insights/the-case-for-stakeholder-capitalism.

decades, the notion that business leaders have an obligation to maximize shareholder value above all else (sometimes referred to as the "Friedman doctrine") endured. It took hold in 1970 after leading economist Milton Friedman said that "in his capacity as a corporate executive, the manager is the agent of the individuals who own the corporation or establish the eleemosynary institution, and his primary responsibility is to them."[2]

I love the word *eleemosynary*," really just a fancy synonym for "charitable." Doing good is so difficult, it seems to imply, that it's just plain hard to spell.

"What does it mean to say that the corporate executive has a 'social responsibility' in his capacity as businessman?" Friedman asked. "If this statement is not pure rhetoric, it must mean that he is to act in some way that is not in the interest of his employers." That assumes, of course, that the well-being of employees, the satisfaction of customers, or the health, safety, and vibrancy of the community are not in the interests of his employers unless these elements contribute to profit.

In his critically acclaimed book *The Heart of Business: Leadership Principles for the Next Era of Capitalism*, my friend and longtime coachee Hubert Joly writes of the "tyranny of shareholder value."[3] Recounting stories ranging from a dinner conversation with his children ("our capitalist system and the way business was operating no longer seemed sustainable") to his own early-career adoption of the Friedman

---

[2] Milton Friedman, "A Friedman Doctrine – The Social Responsibility of Business Is to Increase Its Profits," *The New York Times*, September 13, 1970, https://www.nytimes.com/1970/09/13/archives/a-friedman-doctrine-the-social-responsibility-of-business-is-to.html.
[3] Hubert Joly, *The Heart of Business: Leadership Principles for the Next Era of Capitalism* (Boston: Harvard Business Review Press, 2021).

doctrine and beyond, Joly carefully outlines the circumstances that led to his definitive conclusion that, despite being the wildly successful CEO of a Fortune 100 company, "considering profit as the sole purpose of business is wrong."

Joly is not alone. In August of 2019, 181 CEO members of the Business Roundtable – a coalition that included companies as varied as Apple, Blackrock, BP, Coca-Cola, CVS Health, FedEx, General Motors, JPMorganChase, Lockheed Martin, Microsoft, Starbucks, Walmart, and Zoetis – released a "Statement on the Purpose of a Corporation," which placed four other stakeholder groups alongside shareholders essential to the purpose of their organizations. "Each of our stakeholders is essential," the statement declared. "We commit to deliver value to all of them, for the future success of our companies, our communities and our country."[4]

These groups – customers, employees, suppliers, and communities – became the focus of this stakeholder capital-ism in a way that had not existed previously. The statement acknowledged the criticality of corporate activities once seen as peripheral to the core obligations to shareholders, things like training, education, and development for employees; building ethical bilateral partnerships with suppliers; respect-ing people; protecting the environment; fostering diversity and inclusion; and more.

In what likely would have been cold comfort to Friedman, the CEOs did not dispense with the criticality of share-holders. "We believe the free-market system is the best means of generating good jobs, a strong and sustainable economy, innovation, a healthy environment, and economic

---

[4] Business Roundtable, "Statement on the Purpose of a Corporation," August 19, 2019.

opportunity for all," they wrote. "We commit to generating long-term value for shareholders, who provide the capital that allows companies to invest, grow, and innovate."[5]

This is an interesting debate that is unlikely to be fully resolved in any meaningful way anytime soon. Right now, the pendulum has swung toward the expectation that leaders and organizations manage the interests of a fuller range of stakeholders than just their shareholders. Whether that continues is likely contingent on whether shareholders are confident that their needs are being met adequately amidst crowded competition for time and attention and resources and, yes, money.

For the purpose of considering your role and role responsibilities, however, what is right or wrong or popular or unpopular or acceptable or unacceptable doesn't actually matter. Those questions are left to the domains of morals and ethics. What matters is who you believe you are charged to serve and whether those people agree with your assessment.

Who You Are Charged to Serve

Who do you work for? It's easy to get glib here. Sure, yeah, you work for yourself. And maybe you work for your family. Or for a higher power. Or for your community. Or for the people! (You might even capitalize some words in that last one.) Each of us who has to make difficult decisions is granted the opportunity and privilege to do so by some individual, group of individuals, or entity who can withdraw that opportunity and privilege if they believe that their needs are not being met or their interests are not being represented.

---

[5] Ibid.

So who do you work for? Is it for stockholders? Clients? The public? Voters? A family? Separate from who you work for, on whose behalf do you lead? Employees? Customers? Geographic constituents? Ethical leadership demands educated consent and thoughtful engagement of the people being led. Otherwise, it's just coercion, dictatorship, or propagation of an ideology. Who is consenting to follow you via their enthusiastic endorsement of your leadership, their reluctant willingness to show up every day, or something in between?

Understanding your role and its requirements demands that you know to whom you are obligated, whose interests you must represent, what the dynamics are among the various parties – particularly when their interests seem misaligned – and what is expected of you as a result.

Stakeholder Mapping

Roles always exist in relation to others. There is no role without a system, and the existence of a system requires more than a single entity. As a result, spending time to really understand exactly who those others in your system are and what your relationship is to them is essential to building clarity about the responsibilities of your role. It's also important to understand the differences between what's on paper about those others and how you actually think of them and interface with them.

Those others are your stakeholders, and while their relative importance to any particular issue may vary, they all have a claim on your time, your energy, your activities, and your leadership. How you engage them ahead of, during, and after a difficult decision tells us something about your priorities and your relative commitment to their needs and expectations.

Taken together, your stakeholders form a network of entities who depend on you and upon whom you are dependent. They are simultaneously the people for whom you work and the people you work for, the people you need and the people who need you.

Let's try to make sense of them with an exercise that requires both visuals and visualization. People generally either love this exercise because it reveals so much more about our subconscious interpretation of our stakeholders and their relationship to us and to each other by employing a very different cognitive approach, or they hate it because they'd rather just look at a hierarchical organizational chart or stop once they've written a list. Especially if you fall into the latter camp, consider how trying a different style of thinking and processing might shed light on loyalties, obligations, and relationships that a linear chart does not reveal and that perhaps you didn't even realize you were holding:

- Think about the constellation of stakeholders with whom you interact on a daily, weekly, monthly, and annual basis. Imagine the list of calls you need to return, a week in your calendar, your monthly meeting cadence, and your annual schedule. Who fills each of these? Who appears in more than one? Write down every representative group (e.g., direct reports, other employees, board directors, customers, distributors, suppliers/vendors, consultants, contractors, investors, media, or others).

- Once you've written down most of those representative groups, review the list, and then close your eyes. Imagine everyone on that list in relation to you and the system for which you are a leader. What image or shape do the stakeholders form? Be creative in considering possible images. I've seen this exercise completed with stakeholder images that look like a football field, a garden, interlocking factory machinery, a landscape, a bull's eye, an octopus, a tree, a constellation of stars, a brick building, recipe ingredients and kitchen tools, a topographic map, and many others. Pick a metaphor that feels comfortable and natural to you.

- Now comes the hard part. Take your image from mental picture to actual picture. On a large piece of paper, draw the image that you've conceptualized – without using words. (Yes, draw it.) Don't worry so much about your artwork.

- Using initials only (no words!), add each of your stake-holder categories to their related image components. Don't forget to put yourself into the picture!

- Step back and admire your artwork. You're no Picasso (but as you'll see, that's probably a good thing).

- Consider: What do you notice? What do the relative size, shape, distance, and relationship of the various parts of your image tell you about how you think of your stakeholders? Who is at the center of the picture? Who is at the outer edges? Who might you have forgotten?

- If you're feeling particularly bold (and followed the direction about not using words in your image), ask one or more other people to interpret the drawing. Tell them nothing! Instead, ask what they see. What does the image resemble? What do they notice about the relative size, shape, distance, and relationship of the component parts? What do they think it means?

- Consider: Who do you think are the most important stakeholders on your original list? Why?

- Based on what you've drawn (and your own or others' interpretations of what you've drawn), what about your picture aligns to your articulation of relative stakeholder importance? What is different? What do those gaps or disagreements tell you about how you might actually view your stakeholders?

- And most importantly, what do your concrete and creative interpretations of your stakeholder list tell you about your role and your role responsibilities? What interpretations affirmed your existing beliefs? What surprised you?

- To whom are you most responsible? To whom do you feel most responsible? When are these the same and when are they different? How do you know?

Socioemotional Role

Your role as a leader is not merely about the hierarchical position that you hold, the power and influence that you wield, the tasks for which you bear responsibility, your engagement with the stakeholders that you serve, or where you sit on the map that you just drew. Every member of every group holds multiple roles within a team, organization, or system, and understanding yours – and the impact of these on others – will enhance your ability to make decisions with integrity even in the absence of full alignment of the triangle's sides.

What is a socioemotional role?

The American Psychological Association differentiates among basic group roles (leader and follower), task roles (the actions for which the individual maintains responsibility and/or accountability, in light of the group's goals), and socioemotional or relationship roles (the support or lack thereof that the individual provides in service of meeting others' emotional and/or interpersonal needs).[6] The first two are typically clearer in that multiple individuals working together toward a shared purpose or task generally need to communicate about these and specify assignment of responsibilities in order to accomplish their goals successfully. It is fully possible – and often a source of conflict – for a group to operate without ever openly discussing its members' interpersonal and emotional needs, which makes definition of socioemotional role more challenging. (Of course, plenty of groups struggle to understand and communicate about their task roles and even their basic group roles, never mind their individual and shared emotional needs and the interplay of their group dynamics in supporting or undermining these!)

The responsible leader who wishes to consider her personal morality, ethical context, and structural role will also spend time unpacking her socioemotional role within the team or group. This task is a matter of understanding the expectations that you feel comfortable and confident to take on in your leadership and group membership capacity, as well as those that may feel less uncomfortable, natural, or appropriate, but that other members may impose upon you or attribute to you, nonetheless.

---

[6] American Psychological Association, "Group Roles," *APA Dictionary of Psychology*, 2020 https://dictionary.apa.org/group-roles.

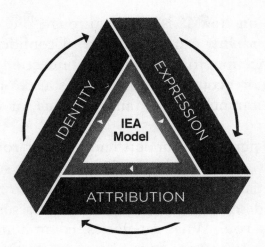

FIGURE 5.1 The IEA model: identity / expression / attribution model of social identity.

Importantly, our roles are not restricted to those with which we personally identify, nor do all of our self-identifications necessarily play a part in how others see us. Using a framework from the field of diversity, equity, and inclusion, we must recognize that there are three dimensions to social identity role: how we think of ourselves (identity), what we show to others (expression), and how others see us (attribution), regardless of whether these align exactly (Figure 5.1).

In the mid-to-late 1970s, social psychologist Henri Tajfel introduced the notion of social identity theory, the idea that our sense of self is shaped by the categories or groups of which we see ourselves as a part.[7] That sense of self is then enhanced by how we see or experience those groups in relationship to other individuals and groups.

---

[7] See Henri Tajfel, "Social identity and intergroup behaviours," *Trends and Developments*, April 1, 1974, 65–93, and Henri Tajfel, et al., "An integrative theory of intergroup conflict," *Organizational Identity: A Reader*, 1979, 56–65.

Depending on how it is meted through one's individual psychology, *identity* can be a source of confidence or self-belief, connection to community, connection to history, pride, and more; conversely, it can be a source of superiority or bias, disenfranchisement, anger, shame, or internalized oppression.

For the purpose of understanding your role responsibilities, knowing and understanding your core social identities is essential. How do you see yourself? How would you identify or describe yourself as a person to someone who didn't know you? What categories, communities, groups, social strata, do you see yourself as a part of? If you were writing a comprehensive identity checklist where you would check all of the boxes, what boxes would be on that list?

Juxtaposed with identity is *expression*, or what we choose to show to others. Sometimes social identity expression is by choice (I can decide whether I wish to tell others about things like faith identity and affiliation, experience as a military veteran, health or ability status, gender identity or sexual orientation, age, country of origin, for instance) and sometimes aspects of my identities may be evident to others whether or not I wish to show these.

In considering your role, it is critical to know what identities you show to others and how you do so, whether those methods of expression are voluntary or involuntary and intentional or unintentional, and what identities you choose to keep to yourself. The alignment and/or gap between how you see yourself and how you decide to let others experience you inevitably affects the way that others will relate to you in light of their own social identities. That expression can help others to answer important questions that inform how they experience your decisions. They might wonder: Are we part of the same social identity group? Do aspects of your social identities enable you to have empathy for my experiences, whether or not we are part of the same social identity group(s)? Do your decisions reflect the integrity of what you have told or shown me about who you are? And how do your answers to each of these questions encourage me to support or undermine your decisions? Can I stand behind you when you make a tough call based on what you show me about how you see yourself and how those identities affect your choices?

Of course, how we see ourselves and what we show to others may or may not bear any relationship to how others see us. Inspired by Andy Houghton, an insightful executive coach and mentor from Edinburgh, Scotland (and one of my predecessors as CEO of our firm), I often ask the leaders who I coach how other people get them wrong.

Think about it for a moment: How do other people get you wrong? And how do those mistakes affect how they interact with you?

The most frequent answers that I get from public company CEOs are that they are excessively ambitious, that they are harsh or demanding, or that they are lacking in compassion or empathy. Few, if any, see themselves in any of these ways. But they generally recognize that their self-concept doesn't necessarily matter as much as how others experience them: "Perception is reality" may be a cliché, but it is a notion that also bears truth.

With regard to social identity, I have worked with leaders at all levels of organizations around the world whose racial or ethnic identities don't align to what others perceive; whose gender identities are incorrectly attributed based on their name or appearance; who have transcended socioeconomic class throughout the course of their careers but who still have a stronger psychological identification with their origins than with their current realities.

It is important to remember that *attribution*, how others see and experience us and how they interact with us as a result, may or may not bear any relationship to how we see ourselves, but it nonetheless has a profound effect on our leadership, how our decisions are received, and even our lives and well-being. The Movement for Black Lives has reminded us time and again that Black boys and men who have perceptions of threat attributed to them because of others' racism experience disproportionate violence and death – including at the hands of those charged with protecting them.

Fostering strong self-awareness is one way to build our ability to understand others' attributions, enabling us to spot and name the identities, characteristics, and perspectives that others assign to us (correctly or not). As we seek to develop our own self-awareness, especially in new contexts or environments, an interview-based 360-degree feedback survey often marks an opportunity to cultivate richer understanding of others' attributions to us. Or, as C.C. Bloom (Bette Midler) demands in the 1988 film *Beaches*, "That's enough about me; let's talk about you. What do you think of me?"

Our roles are not only defined by social identity, expression, and attribution, however. They are also shaped and informed by interpersonal dynamics – which may or may not connect to those social categories. In considering your socioemotional role, you must also entertain what consequent classifications your identified role(s) bestow upon others in the dynamic, team, or system. For instance, if you hold the role of expert or a teacher, someone else is a student or a learner. If you represent a parent, someone else represents a child. If you hold the role of caregiver, someone else is expecting to be cared for. If you are inspirer-in-chief, one or more other members of the group might hold the role of keeping the group grounded and practical. If you are a member of a historically dominant social identity group, individuals who do not share those identities might experience marginalization in their experience of and/or with you.

These three categories – identity, expression, and attribution – don't exist independent of one another. They are, instead, entirely interdependent. How I see myself (and how I feel about how I see myself) affects what parts of my identities I choose to express and how I choose to do so. What I choose or cannot choose to express affects what people attribute to me and how they interact with me as a result. And what others attribute to me and how they interact with me as a result affects how I see myself – and so on. This triangle is, in fact, a cycle.

Keep in mind that if you are not happy with one or more roles that are ascribed to you by others, one approach to reducing their impact is to operate firmly and with clear boundaries in the roles that you wish to maintain. We can't tell others how to see us, but we can behave in ways that reflect integrity in aligning our individual identities and expression of those identities, thereby – sometimes – moving others' attribution to match more closely how we see ourselves.

Now, that's unlikely to be a successful strategy when we bear the weight of historic oppression against our social identities, especially when the collective cultural narrative about our marginalized identities is dominated by negativity and stereotypes. Nonetheless, there is an important mindset that sits right at the center of the approach. In the words of renowned cultural fluency expert Valarie A. Chavis, "Don't chase the lie." That is, reject the incorrect assumptions, stereotypes, and false interpretations that others make based on your identities. Rather than attempting to disprove them, be aware of how they see you but focus on being exactly who you are – bigger and better than ever. In their seminal 2000 article on leadership for *Harvard Business Review*, "Why Should Anyone Be Led by You?," Gareth Jones and Rob Goffee sum it up succinctly: "Be yourself – more – with skill."[8]

Understanding Dynamic Roles

In chemistry, systems experiencing change achieve equilibrium once no more change can happen. That is, there is no more transfer of energy in either direction within the systems and there is no driving force from the outside; until then, they seek equilibrium by balancing out existing forces in one direction or the other.

The same is true in human systems. Driving forces are counterbalanced by restraining forces, and although our tendency is to increase driving forces to enable change, it is often easier to release restraining forces, thereby creating room for more drive with less resistance.

Accordingly, as you dial up the driving forces from your role, you will encounter greater pushback from those who see their own role responsibilities – task or psychodynamic – as being in opposition to yours. The opportunity, then, is to consider the shared purpose for which you are working – the

[8] Robert Goffee and Gareth Jones, "Why should anyone be led by you?," *Harvard Business Review*, September–October 2000.

role responsibilities that overlap even where your roles exist in part to enable healthy equilibrium via constructive conflict in the system.

An easy example: Most organizational leadership teams are designed to achieve systemic goals by creating role conflict. Most leaders of profit centers in business have ideas about how they could generate more revenue by spending more – perhaps not right away, but certainly over time with the right investment, even where that investment erodes margin in the short-term. And while chief financial officers know that margin can be managed via careful cost controls, they also recognize that businesses do not grow via said careful cost controls. The P&L leaders want to spend more; the financial officers want greater prudence – but both want to grow the top line and the bottom line of the business. Their roles and related driving forces start from different points and serve different needs; together, though, they create equilibrium in the system in service of overlapping role responsibilities and shared goals.

As you review the group, task, and socioemotional roles that you hold as a leader, consider who in your system offsets those roles, how they do so, and what prompts an increase in their expression of counterbalancing forces. Do you work in tandem with one another to achieve equilibrium on behalf of the total system, or do you work in conflict with one another to assert your respective individualized roles?

1. **Saver vs. investor.** When you are the *saver*, who contemplates investments in the future? When you are the *investor*, who holds financial caution and security for the system?

2. **Peacemaker vs. provocateur.** When you act as *peace-maker*, who helps the system to avoid groupthink? When

you are a *provocateur*, who helps to ensure reasonable harmony across the system?

3. **Visionary vs. pragmatist.** When you are at your most *visionary*, who keeps the system grounded in the realities of the day-to-day? When you are the *pragmatist*, who holds the sense of wonder and possibility for the system?

4. **Skeptic vs. cheerleader.** When you hold the role of healthy *skeptic*, who provides the group with inspiration and support? When you are the *cheerleader*, who balances your enthusiasm with thoughtful questioning and challenge?

5. **Pilot vs. ground control.** When you act as *pilot*, who alerts the team to potential obstacles or the need for adjustments in your flight path? When you play the role of *ground control*, who flies the plane forward in response to your careful operational direction?

6. **Learner vs. teacher.** When you operate from a position of curiosity and act as *learner*, who introduces experience and expertise? When you are the *teacher*, who absorbs your ideas and thinking and considers how to grow and develop as a result?

7. **Judge vs. witness.** When you are in the mode of *judge*, who gathers data without assessment of value(s)? When you act as observer or *witness*, who balances your observation with careful evaluation against clear criteria?

8. **Divergent vs. convergent.** When you are at your most *divergent* in your thinking, who helps the system to narrow down its ideas and focus on their execution? And when you are at your most *convergent*, who opens the funnel of possibility and imagines options without constraint?

As you explore these dynamic roles and their counterpoints, consider when the presence of opposing forces helps the system to fulfill its collective purpose. Who embodies each of these roles? How do your dynamics affect others in the system? Which roles enable you to be at your best? Which roles create limitations on the system? Which roles reflect your highest-order thinking? Which roles represent you acting out against the system?

Difficult Decision: Breaking Thrivent When It Wasn't Broken

With predecessor organizations dating back to the very beginning of the twentieth century, Thrivent has a long and storied history of helping its clients manage their finances thoughtfully via a mix of advice, insurance, banking, investments, charitable giving, and generosity solutions. It's an unusual organization: Thrivent is by far the largest fraternal benefit society in the US and exists to serve both its clients and society. The organization has grown into a Fortune 500 company recognized as a leader in financial advisory, one of the World's Most Ethical Companies, and a company that makes a difference in communities across the country.

Many of Thrivent's clients have been part of the organization for literal generations, with these relationships spanning families, churches, and community organizations. The deep connection that Thrivent's clients feel with the organization often reflects the trusted relationships, as well as the positive impact, that its financial advisors create for and with their

---

(Continued)

clients. With that kind of foundation, making any changes to how Thrivent operates carries risk for its leaders.

Soon after being appointed chief executive officer in 2018, though, Terry Rasmussen realized that she had a difficult decision to make. With the firm in a strong and stable financial position, continuing with a business model that solely relied on financial advisors at the center of Thrivent's relationships would've been easy: They were loyal, dedicated, purpose-driven, and successful. But the organization's clients told Thrivent over and over again that the company needed to prepare to serve future generations. Recognizing that the organization's biggest risk is its continued relevance, Rasmussen understood the urgency of transforming a great current business into a great business for now and the future.

She started by trying to understand her key stakeholders: namely, clients. "Our clients are essential," she explains. "We're a membership organization. We have to make sure we are delivering on our promises to help them use their finances to lead a full life."

"And so I became grounded in the notion of client centricity," she says. "We watched retailers like Target and Best Buy discover that the key to their success was listening to what their client really needs and wants and desires. A decade ago, Target wasn't in the grocery business. But they knew that their key customer would like to go to one place to shop for everything."

"In financial services, it's no different," she continues. "Our clients need more than life, health, and annuity products. They want advice, someone that they can talk to about making financial decisions. We had to create a broader aperture for Thrivent as an organization."

Rasmussen's desire to do right by her clients aligned neatly with her role responsibilities as leader of the Thrivent organization. But there was an ethos that predated Rasmussen's tenure and that came into sharp conflict: Why break something that wasn't broken – especially when the Thrivent business was doing well and doing good in the world at the same time? "After all," she says, "it takes a lot to kill an insurance company, just by virtue of the business model alone. Why would we bother to transform?"

"Early on," she explains, "I heard resistance from people who already saw our purpose as strong and who didn't want to change. There are probably still some people who feel it was working the way that it was. So why we would want to change?"

Rasmussen was undeterred. Deciding to transform required Thrivent to go "from an organization that was, by nature, transactional. We would sell a client a product they needed, and then maybe come back years later and sell them another product they needed. Our financial advisors understood the needs of their clients, certainly, but we weren't consistently sitting down each client in order to deeply understand their purpose and then unpack what it means to build a financial strategy that helps them lead a life full of meaning and gratitude," she explains. "It means going from being a nice company that gives to charity to being a great company that helps its clients to lead a full life."

(Continued)

In practice, the proposed transformation was significant. "For some of our field associates, [the transformation represented] a big change in how they offer products. For [leadership], the change is balancing our focus on outcomes and our rigor around performance. We don't want to lose what matters to us, but we had work to do to focus on our performance."

The right choice was difficult, but it was perfectly clear. To check her thinking and to consider how best to engage her stakeholders, Terry went back to her own moral core. "I grew up on a farm," she says. "I am a product of advice and planning and discipline, which goes to those roots. It was how I was brought up: The right thing to do is to be a good steward of the land, minding the seasonality of it. There's a delayed gratification, yes. There is also disciplined planning, understanding what is important to you, what you value. That transcended for me into the financial world as well. I feel like I get to lead a full life now, and I want to help others do that, too. How can Thrivent as an organization give people the gift of seeing money as a tool to live a purposeful life?"

The company's unspoken ethos of leaving well enough alone wasn't necessarily shifting. "No one said to us, this is a huge mistake," Rasmussen says, "It took a while to truly internalize what it really meant, though." To enhance acceptance of the decision, Terry began to focus more on her responsibility as a cheerleader for the organization. "I had to paint the picture, show how we can impact the lives of millions of people for the better, and get [everyone] excited about the future."

A change in the broader contextual ethic of business introduced a helpful new angle to the organization's acceptance of the decision. Businesses everywhere were talking about meaning and purpose again. "Companies that have the performance but who are [now] seeking purpose often have people who are so focused on performance that they have to figure out how to get their workforce excited in a new way," Rasmussen says. All of a sudden, "it's not only about financial numbers, it's about impact on greater society!"

That can be a hard sell for some, but it wasn't for Thrivent. "We've been at this – [emphasizing purpose in business] – from the very beginning," she explains. "We have this purpose that oozes out of our pores. What we're focusing on now is our performance bar. For us, it's always both – it's an 'and,' not an 'or.' Our people on the phone genuinely care. They love talking to our clients. They are compassionate, and it shows. Our people love offering our products, but they love making an impact in someone's life even more. With us, because of our front lines – our call center and our financial professionals – we have this huge competitive advantage because they are highly relational. One of our values is that we live in service."

"It takes a while to see if a strategy is working," Rasmussen says, "but there haven't been any points where we've since thought this wasn't right. I ask [all of my stakeholders] to help me think about the preliminary indicators that it's going well – what would help you to see that it's really working? And they've given me lots

(Continued)

of anecdotal stories that suggest that we've got it right, even if it's still early."

"We always have to keep the needs of our stakeholders front and center," she continues. "First of all, that means serving our clients and fulfilling the promises we make to them. The governance of those promises we make to clients are led by our board of directors, and our board members are all also clients and they're elected by our clients. This provides a lot of alignment on our strategy."

And what do Thrivent's people think now? "Well, we have a mix of new, excited, purpose-driven leaders who are showing our workforce what good looks like," Rasmussen says. "We have a long-tenured workforce, which is great. Many of them are really excited by seeing the transformation come to life – they're jumping to the bar that's been raised for them. They're growing and developing and getting invigorated by a higher level of performance expectation for all of us."

And what if she had made a different call – or, in an effort to give the decision more time, hadn't made a call at all? "I don't think we would have the caliber of executive leadership team that we have today if we hadn't done this," she says, "They wanted to make a difference, to make an impact, and they signed up to do the heavy lifting of this transformation."

That's not all. "We would've lost clients. We would've been a slowly shrinking organization. That has implications for our relevance and for our talent."

A Role Exercise

To understand your role responsibilities fully and to be able to draw on that understanding in service of making a great decision – especially one that aligns to or at least can be reconciled with your moral framework and ethical context – you first have to understand your roles and their interplay.

It's easiest to define your formal, hierarchical and/or task role(s), often as delineated by your title, so let's start there.

Ask yourself:

1. What is my job title?
2. How does that title encapsulate or inadequately represent my formal and official roles within the group or system?
3. Alongside those encapsulated by my title, what formal, systemic, or hierarchical roles do I play as a leader for the group, organization, or system?
4. What are my task roles? That is, for what specific duties do I maintain ultimate accountability and responsibility?
5. With which parts of these roles do I most identify? What feels comfortable, natural, or like an easy fit to me?
6. With which parts of these roles do I least identify? Where do I distance myself, either in my use of language or my description of my job to others, from these roles? What are some of the reasons for that discomfort?
7. Who are my key stakeholders? How do I know?
8. Is their relative importance to any particular decision generally comparable or are they differentiated based on the specifics of the decision?

9. Accurately or not, fairly or not, what tasks or responsibilities might any of my stakeholders ascribe to me based on my formal, hierarchical, or task roles?

10. What conclusions can I draw about my role responsibilities and how I need to manage them after considering and summarizing my formal, official, task, and/or hierarchical roles?

Next, let's consider your socioemotional roles, including both your social identities and your dynamic roles:

1. What dynamic roles do I play as a leader of or for the system?

2. What dynamic roles do I play as a member of the system?

3. How do I think of myself as a leader and as a member in relationship to others?

4. How might others describe me as a leader of or for the system and as a member of the system in relationship to themselves?

5. Which of my social identities are relevant and/or important to me in considering high-stakes decisions? Which, if any, are decision-dependent, and which always influence my worldview?

6. Which of these relevant and/or important social identities do I openly and confidently express to others? Which am I more cautious about sharing? Why?

7. What characteristics might others attribute to me based on their perception of my social identities and/or the expression of these identities?

8. How do these attributions affect how I see myself and/or what I choose to show to others?

Next, examine the interplay of these roles in preparing to clarify your role responsibilities:

1. When and how does your embodiment of each of these dynamic roles affect your decision-making on behalf of the system?

2. When you are squarely in one role, who can help you to enhance the quality of your decisions by presenting thoughtful challenge?

3. Who counterbalances me? When? And why? What data does that role – or the person playing it – hold about my own role in the system?

4. Which of these roles do I wish to maintain?

5. Which do I think I should break?

6. What are the implications of holding these roles for this group or for the organization more broadly?

7. How could I choose to shift roles and to show up differently for the sake of sharper decision-making?

Finally, let's bring all of this together in service of clarifying your role responsibilities:

1. Based on my group, hierarchical, socioemotional, and dynamic roles, to whom am I responsible as a leader?

2. What responsibilities does the system hold to meet the needs and expectations of those stakeholders? What responsibilities do I personally hold to meet the needs and expectations of those stakeholders?

3. If I don't fulfill those needs, how will others in the system meet them in some other way? If no one else will fulfill them, how do I need to adjust my view of my role responsibilities to match my stakeholders' expectations?

4. In light of my roles, stakeholders, and my aligned responsibilities, what considerations do I need to account for ahead of making high-stakes, human decisions? What do I probably have to leave out?

5. How can I ensure that I am fulfilling my role responsibilities and remain accountable to my stakeholders? How do I stay consistently up to speed on my stakeholders' views and expectations?

Difficult Decision: A Hundred Years of Picasso

In July of 1919, the Ballet Russes premiered a production of *Le Tricorne*, commissioned and produced by Sergei Diaghilev, at London's Alhambra Theatre of Variety – now the site of the Odeon Leicester Square movie theater. This production has a relationship to the firm that I lead: Its sets and costumes were designed and painted by Pablo Picasso in a studio at 48–50 Floral Street[9] – the global headquarters of YSC Consulting for much of our firm's history.

Marked only by a small plaque on the front of the building, this fact nonetheless felt like no small thing for a firm that prides itself on distinctiveness and creativity: the "most important artist of the twentieth century" (according to the BBC, anyway)[10] painted an acknowledged masterpiece in the spaces where today we conduct psychological assessments and advise

---

[9] Nikkhah, Roya, Royanikkhah, "New Exhibition Reveals Picasso's Love Affair with English Style," *Telegraph*, February 5, 2012, https://www.telegraph.co.uk/culture/art/art-news/9061282/New-exhibition-reveals-Picassos-love-affair-with-English-style.html.

[10] BBC, *BBC History*, "Pablo Picasso (1881–1973). Accessed July 2021. https://www.bbc.co.uk/history/historic_figures/picasso_pablo.shtml.

leaders and reconcile budgets and sift through calendars in Outlook. Whenever we could, we took ample opportunity to share this detail as a way of highlighting our desired brand as a consultancy – one that integrates left- and right-brained thinking, one that prizes originality, imagination, and inspiration, one that is built on uniqueness and character and life-history-defining moments. We referenced our relationship to creative genius on materials in our lobby, in business development decks, in recruitment conversations and resources, and more.

After a while, though, we began to understand that Picasso's generally accepted greatness as an artist is perhaps more complex than popularly considered, particularly given his horrific treatment of women. As Editor Julia Halperin writes in ArtNet, "Picasso once took Caroline Blackwood, the first wife of Lucian Freud, onto his roof and lunged at her. Blackwood describes the encounter, and her own terror, in the kind of lurid detail that one can now no longer help but associate with the many exposés on Harvey Weinstein."[11]

Almost a hundred years later, in her acclaimed solo performance Nanette (filmed for Netflix at the Sydney Opera House – just across Sydney Harbor from our Australia headquarters), comedian and performer Hannah Gadsby asked audiences around the world to reconsider the established brilliance of men in power whose abuse of and/or disregard for women and

(Continued)

---

[11] Julia Halperin, "Is Hannah Gadsby, the Comedian Behind Netflix's Viral Standup Special, Today's Most Vital Art Critic?," *Art News*, July 16, 2018, https://news.artnet.com/opinion/netflix-hannah-gadsby-1318442.

LGBTQ+ people is as generally accepted as their contributions to their fields of expertise. Foremost among her examples: Picasso. "[Picasso] said, 'Each time I leave a woman, I should burn her. Destroy the woman, you destroy the past she represents.' Cool guy. The greatest artist of the twentieth century. Picasso f*cked an underage girl . . . I probably read that when I was seventeen. Do you know how grim that was?"[12]

Grim, indeed, and an obvious rationale for reconsidering ostensible brilliance, especially today. But what does that reconsideration change? As Jock Reynolds of the Yale University told the *New York Times*, "How much are we going to do a litmus test on every artist in terms of how they behave? . . . Pablo Picasso was one of the worst offenders of the twentieth century in terms of his history with women. Are we going to take his work out of the galleries?"[13]

The question isn't merely gendered. In a *Radio Times* interview, Dame Judi Dench asked:

"Are we going to negate 10 years at the Old Vic and everything that [Kevin Spacey] did [as artistic director] – how wonderful he's been in all those films? Are we just not going to see all those films that Harvey [Weinstein] produced?"[14]

---

[12] Ibid.

[13] Robin Pogrebin and Julia Schuessler, "Chuck Close Is Accused of Harassment. Should His Artwork Carry an Asterisk?," *New York Times*, January 28, 2019. Accessed at: https://www.nytimes.com/2018/01/28/arts/design/chuck-close-exhibit-harassment-accusations.html.

[14] Judi Dench qtd. in Roisin O'Connor, "Judi Dench Defends Films of Kevin Spacey and Harvey Weinstein Amid Sex Abuse Allegations," *Independent*, June 25, 2019, https://www.independent.co.uk/arts-entertainment/films/news/judi-dench-kevin-spacey-harvey-weinstein-metoo-sex-abuse-allegations-a8973246.html.

Perhaps, perhaps not. But as leadership strategy advisors, we would be remiss if we were not examining the relationship between our identities, the expression of those identities, others' attributions to our identities, and the notion of genius. What does greatness look like? How does a great leader behave? And who is rarely – or never – included among the array of leaders we meet throughout our business globally?

Considering and reconsidering brilliance is our firm's stock-in-trade. We are established authorities in the space of leadership assessment and senior executive development, known strategists addressing inclusive leadership and diversity, respected co-authors of groundbreaking publications on women's leadership, and sought-after advisors to leaders and organizations around the world that are seeking a path to shape the future.

And like most dominant-culture organizations, we are simultaneously part of a system with its own history of misogyny, gender oppression, erasure of LGBTQ+ people, marginalization of people of color and those from outside of the US and UK, and more. All at once, we are collectively survivors, victims, beneficiaries, and perpetrators of gender-based oppression. (Like it or not, anyone who leads an organization or institution of any kind must recognize this truth.) And we grapple with our beliefs about gender, oppression, and leadership – and the implications of these for organizations and leaders around the world – from our global headquarters in that very studio where Picasso worked through the summer of 1919.

(Continued)

So what do we do? "Cancel" Picasso, even though the BBC said he was the most important artist of the twentieth century? Redo all of our materials? Throw away boxes of postcards and brochures and printed decks? Pretend he never existed? Move to a new building? "If these walls could talk" is probably not an ideal commercial real estate philosophy.

Possibly we don't memorialize our intimate connection in a book, but, you know.

In truth, this one isn't really all that difficult. As a business, one part of our role has stayed the same: to use the tools of our creation and at our disposal to highlight what makes us special and unique in service of delivering a differentiated proposition to our customers. Anticipating and responding to our community's expectations of moral leadership is a significant part of our role in a way that perhaps does not exist in different industries, but morally, there are zero questions about avoiding representing ourselves, our services, and our community with people who unapologetically cause deep interpersonal harm.

What's shifted is our collective cultural understanding of the importance of examining the behaviors and choices of artists and leaders of all kinds at the same time that we examine their work. That aligns neatly to the work that we do and the way that we do it.

So instead of touting our association with the person, I'm choosing to share our exploration of the dilemma. What matters more than what we learn about Picasso – or anyone that we consciously reconsider – is what we learn about ourselves. Let's be honest – sharing a building a century apart isn't a huge deal. But for people and communities who have experienced biases within those walls during our tenure as residents, well, how we engage and how we respond as leaders affects their real lives.

For now, we create an expectation whereby each member of our community examines where we hold dominant group social identities, plus how these affect our view of the world, our work, and our perspectives on leadership. We're less worried about Picasso and more concerned with how we contribute to the marginalization of those who don't share our identities in our place of business and in the world more generally. What feedback can we offer about how we can all improve our co-creation of inclusive practices in our own culture, the identification of great leadership, the development of the leaders whose stories we are lucky to hear and whose journeys we are lucky to join?

Key Points

- Roles help to define how people exist in relation to each other. There is no role without a system, and the existence of a system requires more than a single entity.

- Clarifying the requirements and expectations of one's role is essential to effective leadership.

- Stakeholder capitalism repositions employees, customers, suppliers, and communities alongside investors and shareholders as equally critical to the success of an enterprise. That shift affects the responsibilities of the leader's role.

(Continued)

- Understanding the leader's role and its associated responsibilities demands knowing to whom the leader is obligated, whose interests must be represented, and what dynamics exist among the various parties, particularly when their interests seem misaligned.

- The role of leader is as much about relationships and dynamics – or "socioemotional role" – as it is about basic group, hierarchical, and task roles.

- Visual metaphors for the stakeholder ecosystem can help to illuminate less obvious group and task roles, relationships, and dynamics.

- Social identities, the expression of those identities, and what others attribute based on their interpretation of these identities all affect one another; they also inform the socioemotional roles that leaders hold in and for a system. The better these are understood, the more easily a leader can leverage role responsibilities to make difficult decisions.

- In a system, driving forces are counterbalanced by restraining forces. Increasing driving forces enables change, as does releasing restraining forces.

- In a healthy system, role conflict enables teams to achieve collective, shared, or enterprise goals, even when those goals run counter to individual or functional needs.

- To understand role responsibilities fully and to be able to draw on that understanding in service of making a great decision, leaders must first understand their roles and the interplay among them.

6

Using the Triangle to Make Difficult Decisions

Between our moral code, our ethical context, and our role responsibilities, we've now drawn three clear lines in forming our complex decision-making framework. Alas, three lines do not a triangle make: developing deep understanding of the moral, ethical, and role dimensions of making challenging human decisions doesn't, on its own, actually get us to the decisions themselves. Where the depth of self-awareness that we are cultivating becomes useful is in its application of the angles that each dimension creates when aligned to one of the others. To what degree (pun intended) does our moral code prop up our role responsibilities? How is that identical to or different from the angle joining our role responsibilities and our ethical context? (The equilateral triangle is an easy graphic for considering the dimensions, but real human challenges rarely rely on each dimension equally.)

At its simplest, the triangle enables use of the third dimension as a tiebreaker of sorts when the first two present as being in conflict. Your personal beliefs don't match with the responsibilities of your role? Well, what does your ethical context say is helpful or harmful? Alternately, are broader social expectations different from your moral code? Well, what's your job, and what do your stakeholders need? Sometimes, that third dimension enables reconciliation of the conflict. Sometimes it allows for illumination of the underlying conflict and enables the leader to decide readily between the opposing sides.

And sometimes it doesn't reveal the best choice at all. In those cases, the triangle is still useful: It allows for clarification of our decision-making ecosystem (and the associated expectations of that context); it enables thoughtful learning and development for the leader; it asserts the importance of deep consideration of what truly matters to us; and it helps us to consider what to communicate and how best to do so when sharing a decision with stakeholder audiences whose needs and views may also not align.

Decision-Making Ecosystem and Its Associated Expectations

If morals are internally referenced, ethics are externally referenced, and role responsibilities are stakeholder informed, then the decision-making triangle can prompt the leader to look inward, look outward, and look around. Looking inward enables us to understand what each of us brings to a dilemma, how our early influences, our psychology, our inner voices, or our identities affect the way that we see and experience the inputs to a decision. Looking outward tells us what the world (or, at least, our broader operating context) has to say about them, and looking around tells us what our key stakeholders might think. Those three directions cover much of our decision-making ecosystem. As we do not make difficult choices in a vacuum, understanding that ecosystem, making its components explicit, and seeking as much alignment as possible among the components will later support the acceptance of the decision by audiences seeking consistency and integrity of philosophical and operating principles.

Thoughtful Learning and Development for the Leader

The only way to get better at making difficult decisions is to keep making difficult decisions. Practice makes progress, after all. Although the triangle may fail to illuminate the best path forward in one complex situation, using that scenario to sharpen our understanding of each dimension increases the likelihood that we'll be able to use the framework with greater speed and skill in the future.

The Importance of Deep Consideration of What Truly Matters to Us

Use of the triangle framework should make us better at the act of decision-making, but it should also improve our understanding of ourselves. Regularly checking our moral compass against our ethical context and checking each of these against our role responsibilities (and vice versa) reduces the likelihood that we fall prey to confirmation bias, the psychological principle that suggests that we are more likely to spot and register data that supports our existing, deeply held ideas and beliefs. The more thoughtfully we consider evidence of all sorts – not just content that affirms what we already think – the greater the likelihood that we make better-quality decisions that account for the needs of a fuller range of stakeholders. In return, doing so also allows us to further hone our points of view, which can help us to know when we must draw a line in the moral sand. Beware: the get-out-of-jail-free / do-the-right-thing-at-any-cost approach to leadership is one that leaders get to action only once, lest we be seen as making idle threats.

What and How to Communicate to Audiences with Varied Needs and Perspectives

Helpful though it might be, rarely does the triangle enable simple congruence and clean alignment across a full mix of stakeholders (especially since what often leads to a decision's difficulty – and necessitates the use of a framework to begin with – is the potential conflict among stakeholders). Prompting consideration of a variety of perspectives and their motivations, however, makes it easier for the leader to share the ultimate decision in an empathetic way. Choosing one option means not choosing others, and that inevitably means disappointing some people. But using the triangle to carefully explore the rationale for the leader's thinking and to imagine the vantage points of assorted stakeholder groups means that the hard work of finding a way to explain and connect is already done.

Before we use the framework on a decision that lies ahead, let's reflect on a difficult choice or two that you've already made that can help to bring the concepts to life.

First, choose one or two recent major decisions that you found difficult. Ask: Why were these decisions challenging? What were the points of tension or sources of discomfort? How do you know?

Next, without judgment, only observation, ask yourself:

- Where did this decision align with the ethical and moral frameworks and role responsibilities that I've identified for myself?

- Where might this decision have been misaligned? What was the reason for the misalignment?

- Whether or not the decision was fully aligned, where was my communication of that decision aligned? Where was it misaligned? How might someone in a different seat see it differently?

- If I were to make this decision over again and attempt to fully align my decision-making to my ethical and moral frameworks and role responsibilities, what would I do differently?

- Now that I've looked at a real-life decision, is there anything I need to go back and adjust about my moral and ethical frameworks and/or my view of my role responsibilities? How might my reflection inform a different explanation of my morality or contextual ethics? What might I have missed? What might I see differently now?

Next, carefully consider a difficult decision that is or may be coming up.

- First, clarify: What is the decision I need to make? Who will it affect?

- If I want to make this decision in a way that is completely aligned with my personal moral framework, our collective ethical framework, and my role responsibilities, what will I do? What will I need to say?

- If it is very difficult or impossible to make this decision in a way that aligns all of these, what am I willing to sacrifice? Why? What am I never willing to compromise? Why not?

Next, examine the ecosystem of the decision and channels for its communication.

- Is it easy to communicate this decision in a way that reflects the moral and ethical frameworks that underpin it? If not, why?

- In communicating this decision, what do I need to do to increase the likelihood that the intent behind the decision matches the impact of the decision?

- Is there anything else that we've decided to do or not do recently that could seem to contradict the message that I want to send?

- How can I adjust my messaging and communication to more accurately reflect my intent – without unintentionally making the impact worse?

Last comes the hardest part. Engage in rigorous self-reflection and honesty.

- Now that I've completed the exercise, I need to ask myself: Was I being completely and rigorously honest with myself in my earlier articulation of my morality and accepted ethical context?

- Again, without judgment, ask: What do I allow to take precedence? Why? And at what or whose expense?
- This is a crucible point: Do I need to adjust my articulation of my moral and ethical frameworks and role responsibilities to match how I am actually operating, or do I need to adjust aspects of my decision-making and communication to make sure that what I do matches what I say matters to me?

Only when you have used the framework in full, reflected on its use, and checked your understanding of how your intent aligns to (or misses) your desired impact can you begin to improve your moral and ethical leadership. In part, doing so requires repeated use of the principles that you hold most dear. But improving your moral and ethical leadership simultaneously demands regular and consistent reevaluation of your moral code and accepted ethical context. Otherwise, you've gone from being a thoughtful leader who operates with insight, integrity, and empathy to a plain old ideologue.

The Tissue Test

Is it part of your role responsibilities to be nice?
Is it moral to be nice?
Is it ethical to be nice?
Seems like a strange set of questions, I'm sure, but I think the answers depend on the difference between niceness and kindness.

In *The Heart of Business*, Hubert Joly writes about a few of the reasons why I'd diagnosed his executive team as a collection of A players rather than an A team. "Caretaking was valued over caring," he explains. "This is a subtle but crucial distinction. People were [nice] to a fault, so they avoided delivering hard messages rather than risk hurting a colleague's feelings."[1]

Caring, which is about genuine kindness, involves showing compassionate attention to others. Caring reflects authentic respect for the other person; it therefore demands candor, which sometimes requires telling people things that are hard to hear. Caretaking, on the other hand, is about looking after someone else, about protecting them from emotional or physical harm (imposed by others or self-inflicted). In the parlance of transactional analysis, as explained in Eric Berne's *Games People Play*, caretaking can be described a parent–child activity, one that distances people from each another rather than bringing them closer together as whole adults.[2] Caretaking is undoubtedly polite, and it is certainly nice, but it is not especially kind.

The easiest way to distinguish between caring and caretaking is the tissue test. Do you tell the person sitting across from you that they are visibly in need of a tissue? You might not, lest you embarrass them. It might also be pretty awkward for you! Why bother when you can instead ignore the whole scene? Maybe then their feelings won't be hurt. That's caretaking.

Genuine *caring* would require you to let them know that they need a tissue right away in a direct, clear, unemotional, and nondramatic way – you know, adult to adult. It might be uncomfortable for a minute, but were the situation reversed,

[1] Hubert Joly, *The Heart of Business: Leadership Principles for the Next Era of Capitalism* (Boston: Harvard Business Review Press, 2021).
[2] Eric Berne, E. *Games People Play: The Basic Handbook of Transactional Analysis* (New York: Ballantine Books, 1964).

you'd most assuredly want them to tell you. That may or may not be nice, but it's decidedly kind.

There are cultural elements to all of this; some cultures prioritize decorum or etiquette, collective expectations of behavior, overdirectness, and candor. Keep in mind that just as rules about manners are not culturally agnostic, neither are they morally agnostic.

So, is it immoral to be nice? More specifically, is it wrong to protect people from harm, self-inflicted or otherwise? Probably not. Is it unethical – generally bad in your context – to caretake people? Also probably not. And in your role, are you responsible for being nice to people? Three for three: no.

But we can easily see that it is more moral to be kind than nice and that it is an even greater demonstration of role responsibility to be kind and candid than it is to be polite. Then, ahead of difficult decisions that will inevitably create discomfort for some stakeholders or others, we can adjust our ethical context to indicate that it is always better than not to demand kind candor over propriety and to expect courage over caution.

Triangle Touchpoint: Brilliant Jerks

In nearly twenty-five years of working with leaders across an unusual mix of contexts – and more than a decade of one-on-one coaching and advisory to Fortune 500 CEOs – there is one issue that I have heard raised in virtually every single team in every single environment: what to do about the brilliant jerk. The language varies (Inc.'s Jim Schleckser calls them

---

(Continued)

"cultural terrorists"[3]), although there is greater consistency since Netflix popularized the phrase "brilliant jerk" in an early iteration of its ubiquitous culture manifestos.[4]

The question is usually the same, though: How do I, as a leader for an organization or function, manage an individual whose delivery of terrific performance results (typically measured quantitatively) exists in tandem with terrible interpersonal or cultural impact (typically measured qualitatively, if at all)?

Their behaviors manifest in various ways: sometimes they are flashy and loud, taking the ideas and the air from the room; sometimes they are perfectionistic and manipulative, impressing others until eventually turning on them; sometimes they express big charisma that makes them loved by customers and clients and loathed by colleagues. Like many leaders, I know brilliant jerks because I have had them on my teams, I have worked alongside them, and on more than one occasion, I have been one. (I share that with zero pride, only rigorous honesty.)

My longtime colleague Rosanna Trasatti regularly reminds our clients – and our team – that every dynamic is mutually created. That is, on her or his own, no one individual is solely and wholly responsible for difficulty or conflict in an organizational system. The organizational system and others in it deserve measures of credit

[3] Jim Schleckser, "Why Netflix Doesn't Tolerate Brilliant Jerks," *Inc.*, February 2, 2016, https://www.inc.com/jim-schleckser/why-netflix-doesn-t-tolerate-brilliant-jerks.html.
[4] Netflix, "Netflix Culture," Netflix website, n.d. Accessed August 2021. https://jobs.netflix.com/culture.

and responsibility for allowing and enabling both the brilliance and the poor behavior demonstrated by the individual in question – just as the individual does.

More simply, it's the textbook answer to the classic question, "Why do people behave badly?" Well, because they can.

People who succeed and are rewarded for delivering great results in whatever way they can will do so in the way that is easiest and most obvious to them, often by default. And they'll keep doing it, especially because they keep being rewarded for it.

But why would a conscientious leader – one who recognizes both the brilliance and the jerkiness – reward a team member for a right "what" that is paired with a wrong "how"? After all, underneath, most leaders want to do the right thing. Perhaps we have felt historically that the responsibilities of our roles have required us to subsume aspects of our own morality, and the ethical context that we were operating in and what we understood our roles to be suggested that performance as gauged by revenue and profit was first among not-so-equals. Perhaps that pressure, though officially no longer en vogue, still informs our psyches today. (Perhaps we are lacking in interpersonal courage, but that introduces an entirely different set of challenges.)

Against the triangle framework, two dimensions of this dilemma are initially relatively clear: morally, most of us can readily accept that it is wrong to treat others poorly, especially colleagues. And absolutely, one of our most critical role responsibilities as leaders is ensuring

(Continued)

the delivery of exemplary performance for the organizations and stakeholders that we serve.

As for the ethical context, well, historically, if what was most important was performance, then what people did most certainly was more important that how they did it. In practice, that meant that so long as an individual was delivering, the nature of how they got there mattered less – within the bounds of legality (most of the time, anyway). People identified as workplace geniuses were allowed to engage in behaviors that could potentially be considered immoral – at least, with the benefit of hindsight. And although some of their leaders likely felt even then that the behaviors were immoral, they also likely didn't believe that they would get broad stakeholder support in a broader ethical context where immoral behaviors weren't called out regularly. Perhaps many leaders still feel this way.

The conventional wisdom from management consultants – most of whom never really lead particularly much – or from cultures where cash is not the only or most critical short-term measure of performance – is that the leader should exit the brilliant jerk from the system. Otherwise, that individual will continue to wreak havoc on colleagues' performance and do damage to the collective organizational culture.

If what's prompted the articulation of this perspective is a shift in the larger ethical context, behaviors that are broadly considered acceptable or unacceptable in organizational life today are different than they were even a decade ago. That means that many leaders are as likely to be rewarded or acknowledged for driving exemplary culture as for enabling strong performance; conversely, it means that leaders are as likely to be fired for allowing destructive cultures as they are for mishandling poor performance.

Even so, the impulse to release a top performer for negative behaviors represents a painfully simplistic and not necessarily reasonable view in operating contexts where business cycles are shorter than ever and even limited compromise to performance can have notable ramifications for organizations and leaders. It's not always pragmatic, advisable, or even possible to change out a big deliverer in light of the leader's role responsibilities.

When two sides of the triangle don't readily align (in this case, morals and role responsibilities), we can use the third to make a call between them. But we can also use the third dimension to identify changes to one or both of the sides that would, in fact, enable them to align with integrity. Dialing up the third dimension can reduce or eliminate the conflict within or between the first two.

So what then? Well, with apologies to Ice-T, don't change the player – change the game. If the broader contextual ethics can change, so too can the organization's approach to what constitutes ethical behavior and what does not. The leader then has to override the power of history and the informal cultures and networks that have allowed poor behaviors to thrive – no small task.

Within the organization, ethics are officially communicated through written documents, company

(Continued)

policies, and official statements. More importantly, though, they are informally communicated through systems of reward and performance management, meeting norms and accepted in-and-out-of-the-room behaviors, shadow power networks, and personal relationships that are decoupled from the organizational hierarchy. Addressing all of these issues demands that the leader make a concerted and repeated effort to communicate clear expectations, enroll others who are philosophically aligned to do the same, and create supports to hold each other accountable – especially when it's hard to do.

Aligned leadership doesn't require a difficult decision between retaining the brilliance (the role responsibility) and losing the brilliance to get rid of the jerk (the moral imperative – and probably a role responsibility, too). It instead eliminates this false dichotomy and dials up a bolder, more courageous, and far more relentless communication of ethical context at every turn. The demand, then, from the leader, the team, and the culture, is that every individual deliver both brilliant performance and brilliant behaviors, with a mix of clear accountability and unwavering support from everyone else in the system.

With that approach, the leader's moral code, their role responsibilities, and the organization's ethical context all exist in each other's service, not to reconcile a conflict among them.

Key Points

- It's not enough to understand our morality, our ethical context, and our role responsibilities; making better decisions requires looking at the interplay and relationships among them.

- The moral/ethical/role responsibilities triangle can be an effective tiebreaker in the face of a conflict among dimensions.

- The triangle can also help leaders to adjust one or more sides to achieve alignment across all three.

- Even where the triangle does not resolve conflict or illuminate action, it can enable leaders to better understand the decision-making context, to grow and change, to clarify what matters most to them, and communicate authentically across a variety of audiences.

- Using the framework going forward is easier after taking time to review previous difficult decisions for indicators of clear integrity, indicators of misalignment, and everything in between.

- Leading with integrity demands regularly revisiting the leader's moral code, ethical context, and understanding of role responsibilities.

- Caring is a manifestation of kindness with candor and can enable alignment of the three triangle

(Continued)

dimensions. Caretaking is polite and nice but not kind; it can disrupt the triangle's sides.

- Instead of thinking about how to change out individuals who show up as misaligned, change the system to prioritize both accountability and support for role responsibilities, collective contextual ethics, and the morals that matter most to the leaders.

I Think I Know What I Think; Now What?

Hooray! You've read nearly an entire book – and you've spent countless hours unpacking your moral code, clarifying and considering the ethical context in which you operate, reflecting on your various roles (group, task, and socioemotional), and exploring the interrelationship among these. You are as ready as just about anyone can be to make a difficult decision.

But who said it's your decision to make?

Oh, and what are the rest of us supposed to do? Sit around and watch you make decisions and then live with the outcomes?

Enacting difficult human decisions is more than just a function of understanding where you're coming from, how you got there, and how to reconcile conflict among different aspects of your thinking and your stakeholders' needs. You also have to manage those stakeholders and their reactions to news that may or may not be fully welcome.

Most adults very much prefer that actions that affect their lives and realities are done with them rather than to them. That makes the process of influencing essential in seeing through the enactment of a difficult decision. Engaging people in a decision-making process leads them to feel empowered, but that sentiment can backfire if you're not actually intending to follow their recommendations. People who do not feel represented can and will withdraw their authorization – and your decision, no matter how well-considered or carefully thought-out it may be, will be compromised.

A Decision-Making Process

Here, then, is an end-to-end process for a leader who needs to make a tough call. Now, this process doesn't account for the content and how to evaluate its dimensions; hopefully you've done that already. But before we even begin to introduce the real complexity of a difficult decision to our stakeholders, we need to know how we're going to do it:

1. **Ask yourself, "What am I deciding?"** What is the actual question? Does my framing capture the true, underlying issue(s), or am I considering a superficial question when I really need to go deeper? To go deeper, ask "Why?" As we attempted in Chapter 3, five rounds of "why" questions (the five whys) typically elucidate the real and most difficult challenge at the core of your dilemma. Think through in detail: What is the question that needs to be answered? What is the problem for which you are trying to solve?

Another path into the underlying issue is to consider the criteria by which you need to make the decision. How will you know if you've got it right? What do you need to take into account? If a review of the evaluation criteria indicates misalignment with the core question, then either the criteria need to be adjusted or the question isn't framed accurately. Think, also, about what you want to set aside: What is not included among the decision-making criteria is as revealing about the decision as what is included.

2. **Consider your stakeholder set.** Who might feel that they need to be included or involved in the decision? (And do I agree with their self-assessment?) Who might be interested but doesn't actually need to be involved? Who needs to be aware of the decision? Understanding your array of stakeholders up front will help to determine whether you should even be deciding or leading the decision-making process – which is the third question.

3. **Ask, "Should I be deciding?"** Is this question within my remit? (It probably is.) But even so, is there any individual or team who is closer to this dilemma who might be better placed to make the decision? Is there someone at a lower level in our organizational hierarchy who could make this call without me? If so, why haven't I delegated to them?

4. **Ask, "By when must this decision be made?"** How urgent is this decision? How does the timeline affect the decision-making process? What message do I send by delaying a decision? Keep in mind that the best decision-making approach will potentially shift, depending on

your timeline. Issues with a bigger scope or more importance but without tremendous urgency will benefit from the greater emotional buy-in afforded by consensus-driven decision-making processes; urgent questions will beg more authoritative leadership. At either end of the scale, understanding the timeline will help to inform the answer to the next question.

5. **Determine how the question should be decided.** Should I make the decision authoritatively? Should I leverage others? Do I want to hear my stakeholders' views or give them a voice? Should we decide democratically and offer them a vote, or decide by consensus, and give each individual a veto? The true tests of the best decision-making approach are whether we will be able to decide on time, and whether other interested parties are likely to back the process and the decider(s) once the decision is made (even – no, especially – if they disagree). See Figure 7.1.

That's the first half of the process. Once you've clarified the decision-making process and where the authority to make the decision sits, you need to engage your stakeholder set.

6. **Clarify exactly who you are going to engage and how you intend to do so.** Remember, if you ask someone for an opinion without intending to follow their advice, you risk disengaging or even insulting them. Think through your stakeholders' individual styles and needs and consider what approach will enable you to secure their investment on clear, transparent terms.

FIGURE 7.1 Determining decision-making authority by urgency and desired engagement.

7. *Before* you discuss the content of the decision with the identified stakeholder(s), explain clearly and directly exactly how the decision is going to be made. Don't mess this part up. Avoid the risks of ambiguity or soft-balling the message because you're

afraid that the stakeholder won't like how you expect the decision to be made. They will be less happy if they think they're getting a vote and they aren't. Say, "I'm asking you because . . ." And then specify why you're asking: "I want to hear your view / to account for your voice / to get your vote / or to give you veto power." Make it clear whether you are going to make the call or whether someone else will do so. More on the difference between a view / a voice / a vote / a veto in a moment.

8. **Standardize the process to focus on decision-making.** When I introduced this approach to the CEO and executive team of a Fortune 500 company, they began creating meeting agendas that were organized around decisions (rather than updates or presentations). Next to each item, they identified who held decision-making authority and how the decision was going to be made. Standardizing this process and putting it on paper forced the CEO to consider his expectations of decision-making in advance of the meeting and ensured that everyone in attendance understood and could either challenge or align to those expectations.

9. **Ask your stakeholder(s) for their input.** Be sure to find out why they're holding the perspectives that they express. What is informing their point of view? How do their experiences, roles, identities, communities, cognitive and emotional styles contribute to their opinions? Demonstrate authentic curiosity. Understanding each stakeholder's vantage point allows you to consider implications of the decision for different audiences.

10. **Thank your stakeholders for their input and remind them about how the decision is going to be made.** Say, "I really appreciate your view," or, "Thanks for

letting me hear your voice." Acknowledge, "Your vote means a lot to me and to the rest of the group," or "Remember, if you can't live with this, you have the power to veto it." Don't underestimate the importance of reasserting the process of making the decision and their role in it.

Does the process seem overwrought? This part doesn't even include the complexity of morals and ethics! Why can't you just make a call? On paper, we might appear to be belaboring detailed actions. But in reality, decisions lose their power and their potential for impact when they lose the engagement of their stakeholders. For a high-stakes decision, these steps can still be completed in a matter of minutes. Time invested up front is way more efficient – not to mention more likely to tip engagement in favor of your preferred outcome – than having to repair relationships and hurt feelings after the fact.

If you're going to make a tough choice about a moral or ethical issue, you need people on your side. Start preparing them well before you get to the heart of the matter.

Difficult Decisions: The Best Play for Best Buy

In the world of retail, comps – or comparable sales – are king. Few indicators seem to be tracked as closely or with as much fervor as same-day sales in each store against the prior year – except, perhaps, for quarterly performance. It is rare for one of America's largest retailers to make a major investment in which the effect

(Continued)

on short-term comps is unclear, but that's exactly what the team at Best Buy, led by CEO Corie Barry, has made the decision to do.

Despite facing an unprecedented retail landscape – not only relentless competition from Amazon and other e-tailers, but also the uncertainty and volatility presented by the pandemic – Best Buy has performed exceedingly well. Customers spending more time at home both for work and for leisure have availed themselves of the retailer's mix of products, well-recognized customer service, and variety of fulfillment channels. Judging by the comps and the quarterly performance, things look pretty good for Best Buy.

Why, then, would Barry – a first-time CEO in role for just over two years – aggressively pursue what she calls "far and away one of the hardest decisions we have ever made"? Because aligning the needs of Best Buy's broad array of stakeholders in the context of a still-uncertain future and the moral imperative of a well-defined and beloved company purpose absolutely demands it.

"We're in the process of launching a new membership program," Barry explains, "and it's very expensive in the moment. Not only that, it can contradict some things that we treasure and hold dear in terms of performance management: positive results in the quarter and maximizing results." It's a long-term play in what has historically been a short-term industry.

The idea of a membership program isn't exactly new. "We've been talking about it for years," Barry says.

"We started with Total Tech Support – essentially, a support membership across all of our technology. [Customers] could call, chat, or email, and we would help them. Even then, it was all about bringing more customers into our ecosystem and ensuring that they're using the products. In a more commoditized business, we needed our own unique way to keep the customer involved."

That positive business intent notwithstanding, the results weren't exactly convincing. "There was some uptake," Barry says, "but it was not as high as we would like. And the usage was even lower. It was making money – but only because people were buying it and then not using it. That wasn't doing what we wanted and needed it to do [engaging customers], even though it was profitable. But a change had to happen; we admitted to ourselves that what we had already done and launched just wasn't doing what we wanted."

Reducing or eliminating a profitable part of any business is generally not seen favorably by many stakeholders – especially investors. But Barry and team wanted to understand why customers weren't using the program in the way it was intended. "We decided we need a new function, a customer office. We did a ton of ethnographic research to build out a plan that would do two things: Play to our strengths and give customers what they really want. We learned that they wanted great fixes as well as technical support. They didn't want to pay more money to get things fixed."

Starting with the customer gave the team a different perspective. "Including a warranty is an

(Continued)

interesting idea," Barry continues. "If you have two years of tech support, why wouldn't you buy it?" There were other things that customers really wanted, too: member pricing, early access to new products, longer return windows. The Best Buy team started to model how much those things would cost, and they quickly realized that this idea – prompted by starting from the point of view of a different stakeholder – would be no easy decision.

Naturally, not everyone was on board. "We got lots of resistance," she says. "Internally more than externally. Our CFO was like, 'How do I explain this to investors?' Our chief merchant said, 'So, we do this on top of our promotional cadence? Do I do it just for members? Is it for everyone? What's the impact on gross margin?' Even people who weren't detractors were nervous about our ability to perform in a thoughtful way. 'Can we actually provide this concierge service? Will we be this good?' We had told ourselves stories about how the media and investors would respond. What will they say in the short-term and the long-term?"

"Once we knew all of that," Barry continues, "we realized that if we were going to place a bet this big, we'd have to test it. We started testing Best Buy Beta, combining what we were great at – customer support – and offering concierge support, with the hypothesis being that more people would opt into it and there'd be more engagement, but it would be over time. *Over time* is hard for us, though – we don't have the frequency that, say, a grocer does. We see our customers two or three times a year."

"The decision point in front of us was whether we could build a membership program that people actually love, and would we be willing to take the bet to roll it out nationally?" she asks. "Can we create enough of a hypothesis that there's something here that we'd have the courage to [take this to scale]? Fundamentally, to literally create value for this company in the long term, this is the kind of bet that you have to place to remain relevant to customers. But we'd have to stop building programs just to make money in the moment, and instead figure out the lifetime value of a customer – and then make decisions from that."

A focus on customers and on customer lifetime value still doesn't sound like a difficult decision – but it was the tradeoffs that presented the real dilemma. "It flies in the face of every monthly, quarterly scorecard that we have," Barry explains. "It puts a huge amount of pressure in the system – gross profit pressure, operating profit pressure. These are all things that investors sometimes don't want to hear about in the moment. Even as a management team, we had debate. How do I figure out margin of my products if I have this new membership thing? How do I use it? How does it even work operationally? It challenges us across everything that we do at Best Buy. That means it wasn't just the responsibility of one vertical leader to drive it; we had to think about the impact on every single part of our business."

"I tried to structure us to a decision here by consistently looking at the data with our total executive

(Continued)

team," Barry says. "What is the data telling us? This was our first and biggest bet on data science because we knew we needed the predictive modeling. So we made sure we had the data – but the people part was where it got hard."

"Long-term value creation for the shareholder becomes obvious if we can keep customers and employees engaged," Barry explains. "So we tried to check the box on everyone to see how the proposal would serve across all of our constituencies." The team began looking at their ecosystem of stakeholders in detail. "We started with customers," she says. "This is a customer-obsessed offer. The ethnographic research that we conducted wasn't just asking them what they want – we were watching what they actually do. We could see really clearly both why customers wouldn't purchase what we were already offering and learn what they felt was missing."

"Next it was a question about our employees – but that turned out to be a diamond in the rough," Barry recalls. "If you go on Reddit and look at what our employees say are their worst experiences, it's that they feel that they were pressured into doing something that they don't think has true value to our customers."

The membership offer was different, though; the focus on customers was what persuaded Best Buy's employees. "We could be nervous about the potential financial implications," Barry says, "but we knew that the core of what we were starting to do was resonating with customers. If we get really good at this, our employees embrace it and love it because they see what's great about it for the customer. So changing the customer offer fundamentally changes the employee experience. Our field staff understood that this was a great offer, and that it provided real value to the customer in a way that felt genuine.

"Moving from a great customer value proposition to something that also enhances employee experience," Barry says, "really gives us the courage to do something bold." Who else was in the stakeholder ecosystem? "We wondered about vendors, but they think it's interesting. They asked, 'Could we be a vendor with featured pricing or a member night or early access?' They can opt in, and there are cool ways in which they can participate."

But that still wasn't it. "Then there are communities," Barry continues. "If we get really good at this kind of support, there are concentric circles. Could we offer it to schools? They're working so hard right now to keep every iPad up and running. They need WiFi every day, and if it doesn't work, they're apologizing to parents. There are really interesting ways for us to help communities and the world live their lives through technology."

Even as each stakeholder audience's interests seemed to align, the management team was still uncertain. "We were caught up at the corporate level," Barry explains, "probably because we were working hard to balance both near- and long-term implications."

Fortunately, rather than waiting until the end of its research, testing, and piloting phases to make a

(Continued)

recommendation, the Best Buy management team had sought to engage its board of directors for input right from the beginning. "We gave the board a preview three months in and then dedicated an entire session of the board two months later to show them what we were seeing: way more uptake, and across a much more demographically diverse audience of customers," Barry says. "They also got the data and the testing information as well as our financial forecasts. But even though this is an operating decision, before we decided to go or not, we really wanted the board's advice. And that helped in a different way: They pushed us harder than we'd pushed ourselves. That was the first indicator that people outside of the team would have more confidence than those of us in the building who were working on it."

How could such varied interests – especially against such a big bet – be aligning in such a seemingly clean way? Perhaps, in part, it was because there was another force at play: the company's purpose. "Our purpose is to enrich lives through technology. It always has been," Barry explains. "Even though our founder didn't articulate it in quite that way, it's existed all along. Our vision is that we do it by humanizing and personalizing technology for every stage of life. And if we really believe that, we bring different value propositions to life. Everything we do needs to track back against that."

"Getting really clear on our vision and the cultural and behavioral shifts that would be necessary to deliver on the vision helps to support a big decision like this in a much more fulsome way. We'd have to go from being risk averse to being more risk tolerant, from being customer-minded to being customer-obsessed, from using financial and functional balanced scorecards to prioritizing that customer obsession," Barry says. "This program specifically pushes the envelope on delivering against all of those things."

The moral dimension of the opportunity and its relationship to her role aren't lost on Barry, either. "Sometimes we suboptimize what's right for the customer because there's always another side – trying to make the most money possible. But now, instead, we can say, hey, these are the behaviors, this is how it works, this is what a great interaction looks like, this is why it matters to the customer. If we fundamentally believe in a great customer and employee experience" – and if the team wants to operate with real purpose and integrity – "we would structure all of our decision-making like this to be aligned."

How did they ultimately make the decision to go ahead? "We had a very structured go/no-go process with our entire executive team. We asked, with what we know, do we do this or not? And we were literally voting on it. Of course, my vote is final, and I am certainly shaping my thinking and opinion along the way, but it will fail if it's just me mandating it when it requires everyone to perform in order to bring it forward appropriately," Barry says.

Now, according to Barry, the Best Buy team is thinking about how to bring the rest of the world along – starting with its own people and the investment community. "How do we articulate whether it's doing

(Continued)

what we want it to do in the moment and for the future?" she asks. "We regularly look again at all of the metrics that we're going to use; that way, we can decide what we want to talk about internally and externally and with our vendor partners. And it still makes us uncomfortable! We tried to guess what investors and the media would say – and [Jim] Cramer is on [*Mad Money*] saying this is the most brilliant thing we've ever done."

One might think that this sort of unsolicited support would excite the team, but in the earliest days of so high stakes a decision, the opposite was true. "It made us scared!" Barry says. "We're saying, 'What if we can't deliver? What if we can't do this thing?' Like any big decision, it's all based on a lot of data and a lot of modeling. But it could be wrong. It could cost an investor more, it could not appeal to as many people as we'd hoped, we could struggle operationally."

That's not been the response to the decision from outside of Best Buy. "Sometimes we forget what's special about us. But making this big, bold bet positively reinforces that people want to see us double down on what's so magical about this company. Investors aren't asking whether or not we can do it – they're asking detailed questions like whether we have the right marketing support. They're not asking 'if,' they're asking 'how,'" she says. "Sometimes it seems like the external world understands us even more than we do."

"We know that membership isn't static. We have to iterate on it," Barry continues. "Amazon is a beautiful example of launching and then adapting and adapting and adapting again. Prime is never static. They constantly have components coming in and out. They never touch some things, like shipping, but maybe they'll add videos and music."

"We're really good launchers," Barry says. "We like to launch and then walk away, and that's one of the hardest things about decision-making. There are so few decisions that you make and then you walk away for two years. It's not just how you make the decision in the moment, but how do you nurture and foster and evolve the decision over time? And that means more decisions."

"Already," she says, "we've used this decision to make other decisions. We've announced that for a hundred stores, we are completely renovating them to make them high-end experiences. We decided that we are likely to do an acquisition in health that has some risk and that could have real upside. Each time, we're tacking back to what really matters to us to embolden us to make these harder calls."

"What helps me through this," Barry explains, "is the idea of iteration and optionality. I'm not locked into it as an end state. I need to be agile enough and I need to trust the team enough that we can iterate and alter and adjust – and make more decisions. Sometimes I see leaders double down on a bad decision in and of itself versus just trying to shift and make it better. It's not that our original decision to launch total tech support was wrong. But it wasn't right, either. You can't be so in love with your decision that changing course means you're wrong. You just have to make more decisions."

A View, a Voice, a Vote, or a Veto

Where there is challenge or controversy over decision-making, insufficient clarity about who is making the decision is often a source of frustration or discomfort – feelings that can compromise broader acceptance of the decision, particularly where the decision has moral or ethical dimensions. In an effort to garner broad input or include or involve as many people as possible, leaders sometimes compound the confusion and add to the intensity of emotion around a controversial decision by asking lots of people what they think and then making a different choice.

From small children to experienced adults, everyone loves to be asked for their opinion. Inquiring about my point of view tells me that you care about what I think – and, in turn, care about me. That kind of emotional engagement satisfies the desire to be seen or experienced as significant or mattering, and to be seen or experienced as competent or knowledgeable which, to varying degrees, are basic human needs that we all hold.

But when someone asks us for a perspective and then makes a choice that runs counter to our recommendations, our egos take a hit. Why did you ask me what I think if you're not going to take my opinion seriously? Now, you've gone from showing me that you care about what I think and care about me as a person to conveying the exact opposite. When the decision has moral or ethical dimensions, I've made myself vulnerable to share a personal perspective, further compounding the hurt associated with feeling that my opinion has been ignored or cast aside.

It might seem that the easy solution is to avoid asking for opinions on difficult decisions, but that approach runs directly counter to gleaning the benefits of building diverse teams and engaging others meaningfully. It also squanders the opportunity to begin influencing acceptance of a challenging decision, a process that can begin the moment the question is first asked – well before a choice is made.

How, then, can a responsible leader who wants to solicit input ahead of making a tough call do so without unintentionally disappointing, disengaging, or disenfranchising key stakeholders in the process? Before asking for ideas, opinions, or contributions, *make explicit whether you are offering the respondent a view, a voice, a vote, or a veto*. Absent that clarification, the individual is likely to assume that her perspective is a veto or, at least, a vote – potentially leading to that disappointment, disengagement, or disenfranchisement if you don't follow her counsel.

A View

A *view*, simply enough, is a perspective. When I'm asking for a view, I want to know what someone thinks. How do you see or experience this conundrum? How and why might you see it differently than I do? What should I know or account for from your perspective or vantage point as I'm aggregating data to inform my decision-making? Key here: The decision-making is still mine, but what you think matters to me. Leaders who do not solicit views are engaging in *authoritative* decision-making, choosing based on their own experience, expertise, knowledge, or perspective. Aggrieved parties might call this *dictatorial* decision-making, but there is a key difference: The authoritative leader is granted passive consent of her followers by virtue, at minimum, of their followership – sometimes because of a hierarchical role – while the dictatorial leader may not have that consent at all. Call it authoritative or dictatorial; either way, this model of decision-making positions the leader as sole decider. Oftentimes, the leader has made the decision before she even shares the question with anyone else. Accordingly, a view is not a voice.

A Voice

A *voice* elevates the respondent's input from perspective to recommendation. When I ask for your voice and create space for you to share that voice meaningfully, I am asking not only what you see, understand, believe, or know; I am also asking how you feel or what you think I should decide. With a voice, I am giving you some say in how I choose – but once again, I am still making the decision. Leaders who solicit views but only as inputs and not necessarily as influences are engaged in *leveraged* decision-making; they are gathering and weighing points of view, but the decision remains theirs alone. A voice is not a vote.

A Vote

A *vote* changes the decision-making authority from "mine" to "ours." When I ask for your vote, I am explicitly inviting your opinion with the expectation that it may affect the outcome of our decision-making process. And now it is, indeed, our process; we are deciding together, and each individual's choice will combine to direct us down one path or another. If you're offering a vote, though, you must make additional elements of the process equally transparent: How many people are voting? Is the vote decided by a simple majority? A super-majority? Some other method? What happens if there's a tie?

Voting indicates a *democratic* decision-making process, one in which an identified stakeholder set determines the outcome of the choice together, in aggregate. The rules of engaging in a democratic decision-making process must be clear up front, as this process creates questions for the group and not just the leader. As a voter, what happens if my preferred outcome isn't ultimately selected? What is the leader's expectation of how I will engage with or support the result? These questions are of particular importance in democratic decision-making as – you guessed it – a vote is not a veto.

A Veto

A *veto* moves final authority from the group back to the individual – but not only to the leader: to every individual. An individual who holds veto power can stop a decision from progressing if he is not satisfied with it. This approach to decision-making, also known as *consensus*, requires thoughtful engagement and influencing to align a group of stakeholders whose perspectives, needs, and interests may have a very narrow window of overlap. Accordingly, deciding by consensus requires aligned interests, a strong relationship dynamic among stakeholders, and/or a lot more time. But for a high-stakes decision that is important but not urgent and demands buy-in from the group, consensus demonstrates collective belief and support. It is important to note that consensus does not mean that everyone in the group is happy and in full agreement with the decision; it means that everyone can live with the decision.

Whatever you choose – and you may find yourself changing your mind throughout the course of the decision-making process – what matters most is that you are explicit with your stakeholders at all points about their roles. That keeps the focus on the content of the decision and not on the process itself, never mind a perception of injustice that can derail the entire discussion.

Delegating

Delegating puts the choice to others who have been authorized by the leader to decide independent of her. For delegating to be successful, the leader must first be confident that the assigned decider(s) have the knowledge, capability, and relevant information to make a skilled choice. And second, the leader must agree to support the decision of the delegate unequivocally; otherwise, it's not really delegating, and the leader is still deciding. In hierarchical organizations, more junior individuals often feel responsible for gathering information to present to senior leaders so that choices can be made at the top of the house. Strong systems with clear strategies, healthy cultures, and great decision-making processes turn this model on its head, pushing decision-making authority down as low in the organizational hierarchy as possible (Figure 7.2). In this inversion, more senior leaders are responsible for communicating the

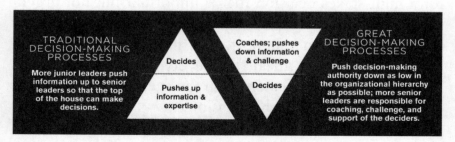

FIGURE 7.2 Inverting the decision-making process.

strategy and vision with clarity and consistency and then coaching, challenging, and supporting the deciders to whom they are delegating.

Sometimes leaders attempt to explore a complex issue without deciding. The intent is often positive: Perhaps I can involve more people this way, I can gather more data, I can avoid making a decision too hastily. But the impact of the leader's avoidance does not always align to that good intent. Not making a decision is, indeed, a decision. The leader who leaves extended ambiguity in the face of a complex conundrum sends a message to others *but leaves that message up to others' interpretation.* Perhaps the leader is inexperienced, incompetent, or overly cautious; maybe they don't understand the importance of this issue and its impact on me and my ability to do my work. Or maybe they just don't care. Left to interpret an absence of information on their own, others are unlikely to come to the conclusions that we want them to.

So what can I do if I really do need more time or more information? First, I have to determine what I would do with additional understanding or time. What content knowledge do I not have right now that would enable me to make a smarter choice? Can I get that information? How? What feelings about the quandary do I need to work through in order to be able to decide confidently? Do I have a context or forum within which to process those feelings? If not, how can I create that context or forum? And how long will all of this take?

Or, as is often the case, am I just using the excuse of time as a way of avoiding making a tough call or dealing with the difficult emotions attached to the decision? In this scenario, the risk of deciding-by-indecision is real.

Facts versus Feelings

Once a process of information gathering is complete – or has progressed to the point of diminishing returns – decision makers need to become sense-makers. That is, the leader or leaders must consider the cognitive elements (thoughts and facts) of the aggregated data alongside its affective elements (attitudes and feelings).

Some processes might suggest that there is value in separating these and focusing only on the facts in service of making the most rational decision. But why is the most rational decision the best decision? Humans are emotional creatures. While mainstream organizational life may diminish the role of the affective domain (and ignore the cultural and gender bias inherent in that view), making decisions with empathy and integrity demands consideration of the total data set – not just its supposedly objective, information-based components.

Instead of separating facts from feelings, consider them together.

1. First ask, "What do we know?"

2. As you (or you and your team) list out the quantitative and qualitative data that you've gathered, check each item for evidence.

3. If you're not sure whether an item is factual, ask, "Do we know that? Or do we feel / imagine / sense that?"

4. Once you've identified a fact, ask, "And how do we feel about the fact that . . ." (Repeat the fact.)

5. List out the most essential facts and the feelings accompanying each of them.

Why is it important to identify both feelings and facts ahead of making a difficult decision? First, within the boundaries of this particular dilemma, neither the facts nor the feelings exist without the other. The fact is a stimulus that triggers the feeling (a response); once the stimulus exists, the response exists. And if a response exists, the stimulus must also exist; the particular feeling necessitates the provocation of the fact.

Accordingly, separating facts from feelings and making a difficult decision with rational information only is akin to using only half the available data. When that difficult decision is a human one, ignoring the affective domain increases the likelihood of causing unnecessary pain via the implementation of the decision. (And you know from Chapter 3 how I feel about causing unnecessary pain.)

There's one more thing: Making a tough choice is typically in service of taking an action or prompting an action. We're not deciding just for the sake of deciding; we're trying to make something happen. That desired action requires initiation of a behavior or a change in behavior, and addressing both the cognitive and affective domains of processing results in greater likelihood of behavioral change than either one independently. Plainly: Accounting for both what we think and how we feel makes us more likely to act.

Tools and Muscles

Plenty of tools exist to help with decision-making processes, but to paraphrase psychologist Abraham Maslow, when all you have is a hammer, everything looks like a nail. Management consultants have long employed responsibility assignment matrices (RAMs) as tools to help leaders and organizations to clarify roles in relation to a decision or action plan. There are tens of variations on these now, but the most popular, RACI, stands for responsible, accountable, consulted, and informed, and designates the part that each stakeholder plays in seeing through a plan to completion. (A recent iteration, "RACIN," clarifies who is "not involved" alongside assigning roles to those who are.) These tools can be useful in organizing work processes, but beware the tail wagging the dog. Assignment of responsibility is not the same as accounting for the full range of your stakeholders, their emotional responses, and their feeling of engagement and authorization (or lack thereof) in an important decision.

Rather than effective use of a tool or set of tools, decision-making is a muscle. Our ability to make difficult decisions sharply and quickly is enhanced by regular workouts to keep the muscle strong, not by ignoring the muscle until we need it and expecting it to do heavy lifting at a moment's notice. We never know when we'll be called on to exercise the decision-making muscle, but strong leadership demands constant readiness to do so. Such readiness requires:

- **Stretching in advance.** Consider the variety of complex decisions that you face as a leader and what makes them so challenging.

- **Consistent workout plans.** Regularly examine the dimensions of decision-making.

- **Variation in areas of focus.** Alternate among morals, ethics, and role responsibilities as your starting point.

- **Built-in rest days.** Plan downtimes with lesser cognitive load and a lower expectation of high-stakes decision-making.

- **Periodic alternation of exercises to avoid hitting a plateau.** Refresh your awareness of the ethical context, clarify your personal morality, and check your understanding of your role responsibilities.

As a relatively square and reasonably studious teenager nonetheless attempting my own version of a rebellion, I responded to an article in the *Philadelphia Inquirer* about the importance of algebra lessons with a snarky and contrarian letter to the editor. (I suspect I was bemoaning poor teaching rather than the entire discipline itself, but I nonetheless naively conflated the two.) To my delight, the paper printed my letter, which ultimately inspired a back-and-forth on the op-ed page. (The news cycle was much slower back in the early 1990s.) The professor who was given the final word shared a lesson that I still carry to this day: Just because football players don't do calisthenics on the field doesn't mean that the exercises don't make them better players.

So it was with algebra worksheets, and so it is with leadership decision-making. The process will come to life at the time of the decision, but the inputs are what make the process strong. Even if you are never asked to share your personal morality, to explain your view of your various roles (hierarchical or socioemotional), or to clarify your understanding of the ethical context within which you are making a tough choice, regular engagement with these questions and workout of these muscles will only strengthen your ability to make the most difficult decisions when you are called on to do so.

Key Points

- Enacting difficult human decisions demands careful communication and consideration of the impact of those decisions on your stakeholders.

- In general, adults prefer that actions affecting their lives are done *with* them rather than done *to* them.

- Even well-thought-through reasoning for making a choice can backfire in the absence of a rigorous process of engaging others in the choice.

- Leaders are as accountable for clearly communicating the process by which the decision will be made as they are for communicating the content of the decision.

- There is a difference between offering stakeholders the opportunity to share a view, have a voice, cast a vote, or exercise a veto; they need to know what they are being offered before the decision is made.

- In an organization, pushing a difficult decision as far down in the hierarchy as it can be responsibly made will increase the likelihood of buy-in from multiple levels of stakeholders.

- It is probably impossible and certainly inadvisable to separate facts from feelings; leaders should instead consider how best to use the logical and emotional dimensions of decision-making to drive desired behaviors.

- Don't be distracted by tools; leadership decision-making is a muscle that requires exertion and regular use to strengthen.

Afterword

There is tremendous satisfaction in making a difficult decision, especially when doing so helps you to clarify what is important to you – what really matters. But there is a shadow side, too. When there is a choice between two compelling possibilities, inevitably one set of possibilities will be appealing or delightful to some people, while the alternative will attract others. What makes the decision difficult is that you are most certainly going to disappoint, let down, hurt, or anger people. For those for whom limiting or eradicating pain is in the moral set (and plenty of others), that is a terribly unsatisfactory outcome.

What's worse: after hurting or disappointing some people, potentially some of your key stakeholders, you aren't even going to know if the decision was right.

In some ways, it doesn't matter. We can never really know whether a difficult choice might have played out differently had we selected an alternative. Even if we change course, the timing is different, the conditions are different, another road has already been traveled.

What matters is that we have made a difficult decision, and we have hopefully done so with intent. Any decision made with intent is better than no decision – or a decision made by default. Even better, we have tried to align our core moral

191

beliefs to the ethical context within which we are operating and tried to align those to our role responsibilities to and with a variety of stakeholders. The process of aligning our intentions has likely made for a better-quality decision, and hopefully one that we can stand behind, regardless of the outcome.

That is not to say that we should fall so in love with our own decisions that we can't see where to iterate or how to adjust. Rather, our responsibility as leaders who wish to operate with integrity, insight, and empathy is to take the deep reflection that we've done ahead of making the tough choice and replicate that process over and over again. Hopefully, we'll get better at deciding even more quickly and even more confidently in the future as a result, all while gleaning even further learning from our reflections.

This meta-process reminds us that leadership decision-making is never a one-time activity; instead, it is a nonstop cycle where each decision likely prompts more still to be countenanced. There are undoubtedly more choices to be made along the way, starting immediately by following the first choice. What will we say? How will we tell people? How will we respond to challenge? What will we do if someone important to us is really upset? And so on.

The process goes on endlessly. Your job as a leader is to affirm the decision you've made – to reflect on how you got there, be clear about what you plan to communicate about both the decision and the process of arriving at it, and know to whom you intend to communicate and how to match your message with their priorities and beliefs and interests.

After that, well, then you can get going.

Making a difficult decision is just the beginning.

Acknowledgments

As a professional ambivert who has returned to my more naturally introverted style, I have very much enjoyed many of the solitary hours of writing that the creation of this work has enabled. But to suggest that I have done any aspect of it alone would be untrue – immoral, even!

I am deeply indebted to my close colleague, professional partner, and dear friend **Steph Komen**, whose thoughtful, interpersonal style, easy laughter, genuine caring, organizational brilliance, managerial skill, and gentle prodding have made it possible for me to write this book.

One of the first difficult decisions that writers make is who will be best-suited to publish their work. Thankfully, **Mike Campbell** at Wiley made that easy with a mix of good humor, challenge, curiosity, encouragement, and support, and **Christina Verigan and Cheryl Ferguson**'s work have confirmed that the decision was a good one, indeed.

I have learned most of what I have been privileged to learn about leadership by being around brilliant and very generous leaders, some of whose experiences are incorporated within these pages. Thank you to **Corie Barry, Ginger Gregory, Kaywin Feldman, Lori Rose Benson, Patrice Louvet,** and **Terry Rasmussen** for sharing your professional lives, your hearts, and your thinking over the years – and for agreeing to share some of your toughest decisions with me and the readers of this book. Thank you, also, to leaders like **Adam Greenblatt, Andrew Meslow, Anna Bakst, Amy Hauk, Chris Testa, Jide Zeitlin, Kristin Peck, Lisa Catanzaro, Marnita Schroedl, Martin Waters, Sarah Dunn, Shari Ballard, Victor Luis, Wendy Kahn,** and countless others for sharing your stories, your dilemmas, and many difficult choices with me. I am extraordinarily fortunate to have learned with and alongside you. I am particularly thankful to **Hubert Joly** for your generosity of spirit, time, wisdom, and network; I may have been the coach, but I have learned more from you in return than I ever imagined possible.

YSC Consulting is a very special organization, and I am grateful to be surrounded by a whip-smart, characterful, and world-class leadership team. Thank you to **Carly Lund, Edwina McDowall, Nik Holgate, Rosanna Trasatti, Sam Gilpin, Shelley Winter, Steve van Zuylen, Tessa Breslin,** and **Yamaris Brodsky** for allowing me to be on this journey with each of you; to a person, you are caring, inspiring, and brilliant. Thank you to our chair, **Richard Atkins**, for your commerciality, calm, and cleverness; it is a tremendous privilege to get to work with you. Thank you to our partners at Graphite Capital for their support of YSC Consulting and of my leadership, including **Mike Tilbury, Rachael Baker, May Sulaiman, Simon Ffitch,** and **Rod Richards.**

My brilliant colleagues at YSC, both current and former, are too numerous to mention, and it feels unfair to leave anyone out. Nevertheless, I would be remiss were I not to thank **Andy Houghton, Anita Kirpal, Ceci Garcia, David Sheingold, Francesca Elston, Neil Jacobs, Rob Morris, Rachel Robinson,** and **Robert Sharrock.** What I have learned from each of you about leadership and decision-making could fill many more books. Thank you also to **Shirley Jaffe, Simon Fincham,** and **Jamie Garrod** for your exquisite designs and tireless work to support the development of this book and all of our work together.

Thank you to **Amy Rhodes, Dana Forman, Donna D'Alessandro, Julia Choe, Katrina Avila Munichiello, Kim Westheimer, Leslie MacKrell, Lorne Behrman, Michael Wise, Ophira Eisenberg, Pamela Sneed, Paul Hirsch,** the late **T'ai Merion, Toni Harris-Quinerly,** and **Wade Davis.** There are pieces of each of you in my heart and in these pages. I am eternally indebted to the educators who have shaped my thinking and my life and who, in many cases, still do. Thank you to **Carmen Pirollo, Cheryl & Jim Keen, Dale Bryan, Doug Upton, Janet Rabin, Jean Wu, Jeanne Dillon, Liz O'Keefe, Lois Horowitz, Natalie Johnson, Valarie Chavis,** and **Vince Perro,** among so many others.

The greatest joy of my life is to be part of a wholly unique, intensely loving, wildly charming, hilarious, and supportive family. Thank you to my children, **Ruby, Jeremiah,** and **Ezra,** and our beloved **Diane and Paul Pliner; Todd, Ashley,** and **Judah Pliner; Sherry Bloom;** and **Deohuttie Hariprashad.** In your own way, each of you helped to make this book possible.

There is no way to ever properly or fully thank my husband, **Jonathan Bloom.** He has helped me to see possibility, imagine a future different from each and every present moment, make many of life's toughest choices, and enjoy the magic of the universe in ways that I'd never envisioned. I could not have written this book – or, really, done much of anything in my life – without him.

And finally, thank you to three very special women who each made one of the most difficult decisions imaginable, affecting innumerable lives in the process and multiplying the love in the world. **Serenity, Jacquelin,** and **Emily,** you are my heroes.

About the Author

Eric Pliner is chief executive officer of YSC Consulting (www.ysc.com). He has designed and implemented leadership strategy in partnership with some of the world's best-known CEOs and organizations. Eric's other writings on leadership have been featured in *Harvard Business Review*, *Fortune*, *Forbes*, and *Fast Company*. A member of the Dramatists' Guild of America, Eric is co-author of the *U.S. National Standards for Health Education* (2005) and *Spooky Dog & the Teen-Age Gang Mysteries* (with Amy Rhodes), an Off-Broadway theatrical parody of television cartoons for adults (Concord Theatricals). He is a board director with Hip Hop Public Health, co-founded by Doug E. Fresh and Dr. Olajide Williams. Eric holds an MBA in management and organizational behavior from the Zicklin School of Business at the City University of New York and a BA in American Studies and Peace & Justice Studies from Tufts University. He lives in Brooklyn, New York, with his husband, Jonathan, and their three children.

Index

360-degree feedback survey, usage, 126

720-degree feedback survey, creation, 72

A

Absolutism, problems, 31

Amazon, competition, 170

American Beverage Association, sponsorship controversy, 85–92

Angelou, Maya, 46

Artist behaviors, collective cultural understanding (shift), 144

Attribution, 126–127
impact, 138
self-perception, relationship, 126

Audience needs/perspectives (variation), communication content/process, 150–153

Authoritative decision making, 181

B

Balance Calories Initiative (ABA), 87

Ballet Russes, Picasso costumes, 140

Barry, Corie, 170–179

Basecamp, political agnosticism (reaction), 93–94, 95

Baxalta, Shire Pharmaceuticals purchase (integration problems), 107–109

Benson, Lori Rose, 85–92

Berne, Eric, 154

Best Buy
board of directors, management team engagement, 176
customers
focus, 173–174
understanding, 171–172
decision point, 1732
employees
experience, enhancement, 175
interaction, 174–175
investor resistance, 172
membership program, difficult decision, 169–179
shareholder, long-term value creation, 174
Total Tech Support, 171
vision, clarity, 176–177

Biden, Joe (ethics-related policies/practices), 96–97

Blackwood, Caroline, 141

Board of directors, chairs (responsibility), 15
Brilliant jerks, 155–160
Built-in rest days, usage, 189
Business Roundtable, "Statement on the Purpose of a Corporation," 116

C
Cancel culture, 84
Candidates, morality/values (consideration), 53–54
Caretaking/caring, contrast, 153–154
Caring, requirements, 154–155
Centaurs, decision making, 10
Chavis, Valarie A., 128
Chief Executive Officer (CEO)
  compassion/savviness, combination (desire), 16
  morality, 16
  options, 13–14
  self-perception, 125
Chief financial officers, margin management, 129
Cigarette marketing/selling, ethics, 76–77
Cigarette smoking, rules/norms/ethics (considerations), 76
Client portfolio, 2
Clinton, Bill (impeachment), 28–29
Coinbase, political agnosticism (reaction), 93–94, 95
Cole Jones, Frances, 7
Collective cultural understanding, shift, 144
Community care, concept (introduction), 20
Community members, harm (avoidance), 5–6
Confirmation bias, impact, 149–150
Consensus, 183

Context, importance, 66–67
Contextual ethics
  alignment, 16
  examination, 25
Controversy, leader avoidance, 13
Conversations, closure (absence), 4
Corporate executive, social responsibility (meaning), 115
Courage/vulnerability, demonstration, 50
COVID-19
  spread, 34–40
  vaccination, US insistence, 21
Co-worker ideas/narratives, organizational practice decisions, 3–4
Cultural bias, 186
Cultural terrorists, 156
Cultures, priorities, 155
Cutter, Chip, 18

D
Daurio, Ken, 81
Decision making
  authority
    change, 182
    determination, 167f
    identification, 168
  challenges, 151–153, 180
  content
    defining, 164–165
    discussion, preparation, 167–168
  controversy, 180
  criteria, 165
  deadline, 165–166
  ecosystem
    clarification, 148
    examination, 152
    expectations, 148–153
  feelings/facts, identification, 187
  focus areas, variation, 188

frameworks
  exploration, 31–32
  formation, 147
  moral-ethical-role responsibility
    triangle, usage, 149–150
  muscle, 188
  positions, model, 182
  process, 11–17, 164–169
    determination, 166
    engagement, problems, 164
    inversion, 184f
    standardization, 168
    tools, 187–189
  question, 165
  time, pressure, 17
  tools, 187–189
Decision transparency,
    appreciation, 40
Delegating, 184–185
Democratic decision-making
    process, 183
Dench, Judi, 142
Dictatorial decision making, 181
Difficult decisions, 8–11
  Best Buy membership pro-
    gram, 169–179
  contagion, containment, 17–22
  Guston, Philip (retrospective),
    National Gallery of Art
    controversy, 60–67
  Hip Hop Public Health
    (HHPH), ABA sponsor-
    ship (controversy), 85–92
  moral-ethical-role responsibility
    triangle, usage, 147–148
  Picasso, canceling, 140–145
  Ralph Lauren workforce
    furlough, 34–41
  Shire Pharmaceuticals, HCM
    software usage
    (controversy), 105–111
  Thrivent, transformation,
    131–136

Divergent, convergent (contrast),
    130
"Do no harm" ethic, 99–100
Driverless cars, development
    (ethics), 78–79
Dynamic, mutual creation,
    156–157
Dynamic roles
  consideration, 138
  understanding, 128–131

E
Ego, hit, 180
Election (Payne), 27–29
Eleemosynary, difficulty, 115
Empathy, usage, 186
Ethics, 12, 75
  change, 77, 81–83
  characteristics, 77–85
  coexistence, 83
  context
    consideration, 122, 163
    shift, 158–159
    understanding, 80
  contextual dependence, 77–81
  exercise, 102–104
  frameworks, 77–78
    learning, 102–103
  judgment, relationship,
    100–102
  morals, conflict, 23–24, 27–29
  reflection questions, 104
  rules, exceptions, 97–100
  shared social acceptability,
    relationship, 77, 83–85
  waiving, 95–100
Expression, 126–127
  identity, contrast, 124

F
Facts, feelings (contrast), 186–187
Falwell, Jerry, 44
Feldman, Kaywin, 60–67

Financial performance, values (relationship), 6
Five whys, 68–70
Followers, group (APA differentiation), 122
Fox News, sponsorship withdrawals, 93
Free-market systems, value, 116–117
Fresh, Doug E., 86
Friedman doctrine, 115–116
Friedman, Milton, 115, 116

G
Gadsby, Hannah, 141–142
Games People Play (Berne), 154
Gender bias, 186
Gender oppression, 143
Georgia voting laws, boycotts, 93
Goffee, Rob, 128
Good decisions, perception, 11
Gregory, Ginger, 105–111
Groupthink, avoidance, 129–130
Guston, Philip (retrospective), National Gallery of Art controversy, 60–67

H
Halperin, Julia, 141
Heart of Business, The (Joly), 115, 153
High-stakes decisions, buy-in (demand), 183
Hill, Anita, 29
Hip Hop Public Health (HHPH), ABA sponsorship controversy, 85–92
Hiring manager, role (demands), 14–15
Hollman Keen, Cheryl, 33
Honesty, engagement, 152–153
Hope, focus, 39–40
Houghton, Andy, 125
How to Wow (Cole Jones), 7

Human capital management (HCM) system usage (controversy), 105–111
Human decisions, enacting (difficulty), 163–164
Human objectivity, nonexistence, 10

I
Identity/expression/attribution (IEA) model of social identity, 123f, 126–127
In-and-out-of-the-room behaviors, 160
Integrity, impact, 186
Interpersonal dynamics, 126–127
Interview-based 360-degree feedback survey, usage, 126

J
Job
  role, contrast, 113
  serving/server, identification, 117–131
  title, defining, 137
Joly, Hubert, 115–116, 153
Jones, Gareth, 128
Judge, witness (contrast), 130
Judgment
  definition, 101
  ethics, relationship, 100–102
  reliance, 10–11

K
Keen, Jim, 33
KKK imagery, impact, 61–67

L
Leaders
  alignment/defense, decision, 46–47
  assistance, opportunities, 3

behaviors, 156
    collective cultural under-
        standing, shift, 143
brilliant jerks, 155–160
choices, consequences, 15–16
conflicts, 24–25
decisions, complexity/
    difficulty, 7, 41
group, APA differentiation, 122
morality/role responsibilities,
    conflict, 4–5
negative behaviors, release
    (impulse), 159
objective information, usage, 11
quit/leave option, 26
role, responsibilities (under-
    standing), 12
socioemotional role
    review, 129–130
thoughtful learning/devel-
    opment, 149
views, solicitation, 182
Leadership
    alignment, brilliance
        requirement, 160
    contexts, morality (applica-
        tion), 49–50
    decision, ethics/morals, 12
    decision making, 189
    dilemmas, 5
    interpersonal characteristic, 9
    journey, map (drawing
        exercise), 73
    narrative, exercise, 70–73
    readiness, demand, 188–189
    role requirements/expectations,
        clarification (impor-
        tance), 113–114
    servant leadership, 114
    strategists, work (impact), 2–3
    styles, intentional design
        (ensuring), 6
    tough choices, relationship, 9–10

Learner, teacher (contrast), 130
Let's Move initiative (Obama), 86
Leveraged decision making,
    engagement, 182
LGBTQ+, erasure, 143
Lifetime achievement award,
    introduction creation
    (exercise), 71
Louvet, Patrice, 35–40

M
Marketing focus group,
    exercise, 72
Mayer, Musa, 62
Memorial service speech,
    exercise, 71
Message, interpretation, 185
Misérables, Les (Hugo), 30–31
Misogyny, 143
Mistreatment, moral perception,
    157–158
Moral code, impact, 147–148
Moral compass, checking, 149–150
Moral-ethical-role responsibility
    triangle, 23, 24f
    alignment, absence, 121
    misalignment, 159
    practicality, 26–27
    touchpoint, 155–160
    usage, 147–148
    values conflict, 51–54
Morality
    baseline, clarity, 45–46
    communication, 47–50
    exercise, 70–73
    parameters/boundaries,
        understanding, 56–60
    sources, knowledge, 54–60
Moral leadership narrative/brand,
    elucidation (exercises),
    71–73
Moral Majority, cultural
    dominance, 44–45

Morals, 12, 43
  clarity, assumption, 51
  consideration, 103
  ethics, conflict, 23–24, 27–29
  exercise, 67–70
Movement for Black Lives, impact,
  126

N
National Gallery of Art, Philip
  Guston retrospective
  (controversy), 60–67
Negativity, impact, 127–128
Nonmaleficence/beneficence,
  combination, 99

O
Obama, Barack (ethics policies
  waivers), 96
Obama, Michelle, 86
Operating context, change, 12–13
Opinion
  asking, avoidance, 180–181
  engagement, 166
Organizational leadership team
  achievements, 129
Organizations
  assistance, opportunities, 3
  contract, acceptance
    (dilemma), 7–8
  leadership dilemmas, 5
  values/morals communication,
    52

P
Pain
  avoidance, 58
  infliction, minimization, 59
Partnership for a Healthier
  America, 86
Patagonia, partisan politics
  accusation, 94

Paul, Cinco, 81
Payne, Alexander, 27
Peacemaker, provocateur
    (contrast), 129–130
Perception, reality (equivalence),
    125
Performance, short-term measure,
    158
Personal beliefs, role
    responsibilities
    (matching), 148
Personal morality, consideration,
    122
Personal morals, perception,
    14–15
Personal relationships,
    organizational hierarchy
    decoupling, 160
Picasso, canceling (difficult
    decision), 140–145
Pilot, ground control (contrast),
    130
Political agnosticism, 93–95
Political correctness, 84
Political leadership, ethics, 92–95
Project/account, participation
    (exit option), 3
Proposal, proofreading, 2

Q
Question, decision process (deter-
    mination), 166

R
Ralph Lauren, workforce furlough
    (decision difficulty),
    34–41
Rasmussen, Terry (difficult
    decision), 132–136
Recommendations, ignoring, 180
Responsibility assignment matrices
    (RAMs), usage, 188

Responsible, accountable,
     consulted, and informed
     (RACI), 188
Responsible, accountable, con-
     sulted, informed, and not
     involved (RACIN), 188
Revenue, rejection (dilemma),
     4–6
Reynolds, Jock, 142
Right thing, constitution, 42
Right/wrong
   baseline, 45
   consideration, absence, 103
   religion, impact, 55
Roles
   boundaries, clarity, 127
   consideration, 124–125
   defining, 126–127
   driving forces, 128–129
   dynamic roles, understanding,
      128–131
   exercise, 137–140
   existence, 118
   job, contrast, 113
   requirements/expectations,
      clarification (impor-
      tance), 113–114
   responsibilities, 113, 124, 147
      clarification, 139–140
      moral compass, check-
         ing, 149–150
      personal beliefs,
         matching, 148
   serving, identification, 117–131
   socioemotional role, 121–128
   structural role, consid-
      eration, 122

S
Saver, investor (contrast), 129
Schleckser, Jim, 155
Schmigadoon (Daurio/Paul), 81

Self-assessment, agreement
     (question), 165
Self-awareness, fostering, 126
Self-determination, increase, 84
Self-perception, 125
   attribution, relationship, 126
Self-reflection, usage, 152–153
Sense-makers, becoming, 186
Servant leadership, 114
Service providers, morality/
     role responsibilities,
     4–5
Serving
   identification, 117–131
Shadow power networks, 160
Shareholder
   long-term value creation, 174
   value, tryanny, 115–116
Shareholders
   core obligations, 116
Shire Pharmaceuticals, human
     capital management
     (HCM) system
     usage (controversy),
     105–111
Skeptic, cheerleader
     (contrast), 130
Smee, Sebastian, 64
Social desirability, risk, 102
Social identity, 126–127
   consideration, 138
   historic oppression, 127–128
   identity/expression/attribution
      (IEA) model, 123f
   theory, 123–124
Social responsibility, meaning, 115
Socioemotional role,
     121–128
   consideration, 138
   definition, challenge, 122
   leader review, 129–130
Spacey, Kevin, 142

Stakeholders
  alignment, absence, 26
  capitalism, 114
  conflict, 150
  decision content, discussion
      (preparation), 167–168
  exercise, 119–121
  identification, 137
  identity-related marginalization,
      93
  input
      request, 168
      thanking, 168–169
  leader obligation, 13
  mapping, 118–121
  repositioning, 114–115
  set, consideration, 165
  styles/needs, consideration, 166
  subconscious interpretation, 119
"Statement on the Purpose of a
      Corporation" (Business
      Roundtable), 116
Stereotypes, impact, 127–128
Structural role, consideration, 122
Systemic goals, organizational
      leadership team
      achievement, 129

T
Tajfel, Henri, 123
Teams
  assistance, opportunities, 3
  members, leader reward
      (reason), 157
Thomas, Clarence, 29
Thoughtful learning/development,
      149
Thrivent, transformation (difficult
      decision), 131–136
Tissue test, 153–155
Total data set, consideration, 186
Tough choices

  leadership, relationship, 9–10
  usage, 187
Trasatti, Rosanna, 156
Trump, Donald
  ethics rules/requirements,
      changes, 96
  moral leader self-perception, 48
Tucker Carlson Tonight, sponsorship
      withdrawals, 93

V
Values, 43–44
  clarity, assumption, 51
  conflict, 51–54
  shareholder value, tyranny,
      115–116
Veto, 180, 183–184
View, 180, 181–182
Visionary, pragmatist (contrast),
      130
Voice, 180, 182
Vote, 180, 182–183

W
Waivers, granting (reasons), 97
Walker, Darren, 65
Weinstein, Harvey, 141, 142
White Lotus, The (White), 30–31
White, Mike, 30
Williams, Olajide, 86
Win as Much as You Can
      (WAMAYC), 32–34
Winfrey, Oprah, 46
Wokeness, 84
Work
  impact, meaningfulness, 5–6
  responsibility, identification,
      117–131
Worker well-being, care (moral
      obligation), 19
Workout plans, 188
Worldview, clarification, 70–71